THE SPIRITUAL LIFE

Learning East and West

THE SPIRITUAL LIFE

Learning East and West

John H. Westerhoff III
AND
John D. Eusden

THE SEABURY PRESS · NEW YORK

1982
The Seabury Press
815 Second Avenue
New York, N.Y. 10017

Printed in the United States of America

Library of Congress Cataloging in Publication Data

Westerhoff, John H.
    The spiritual life.

    Bibliography: p. 133
    1. Spiritual life. 2. Religions. I. Eusden,
John Dykstra.   II. Title.
BL624.W43   248.4   81-21312
ISBN 0-8164-0516-6   AACR2

We dedicate this book to
our families, students, colleagues, and friends
who have shared our journey and helped us along the way

Contents

CHAPTER ONE

Conversations
Christian Life
in a Connected World

We, the authors of this book, John Westerhoff and John Eusden, first met and got to know each other in the 1960s. During the ensuing years our journeys went in different directions, but in search of common ends. Now our paths have once again crossed, and this book is the fruit of a dialogue about those journeys. We hope that in sharing our exchange, we can be of help to others.

In the late 1960s both of us were ministers in the United Church of Christ; had been educated at Harvard and Yale, and were deeply rooted in a Congregational, Puritan, Calvinist heritage. We were living and working in western Massachusetts. One of us was pastor of the First Congregational Church in Williamstown (United Church of Christ), the other was chaplain and professor of religion at Williams College. During the following years one of us focused his ministry on parish religious education, the other on the college chaplaincy and the teaching of religion to undergraduates. More important, while engaged in these pursuits, both of us found ourselves in search of an affective, spiritual dimension for our own lives, a sense of wholeness different from and to be placed alongside our shared tradition—a perspective always being refined by our differing pursuits. In searching for a new spiritual dimension, one of us turned to the Catholic tradition—east and west—the other turned to Eastern religions, particularly Taoism and Mahayana Buddhism. Today one finds himself an Episcopal priest whose greatest satisfaction comes from teaching spirituality, catechetics, liturgy, and spiritual direction in an ecumenical divinity school; the other, while continuing strong connections with the Congregational church (U.C.C.), devotes himself, as a full-time teacher, to engaging college students in a reflective study of the nature of religion and of the religions of East Asia.

Aware that our differing pilgrimages, but common quest, are shared by an increasing number of Christians, we united our efforts to offer this book on the spiritual life—on learning East and West and its implications for Christian nurture or catechesis. Each of us has written out of his own personal experience and conviction, yet we do so from a common perspective and a number of shared convictions.

At the center of all human life is the quest for the integration of the material and the nonmaterial, the body and the soul, the secular and the sacred. Spirituality has to do with being an integrated person in the fullest sense. We humans seem to know that we are more than physical bodies and intellects, that our environment is more than the physical universe known only indirectly through sense experience, and reason. We seem to grasp that we are also spiritual beings and that our universe is also comprised of a nonphysical, spiritual dimension which can be known directly by encounter and participation.

That explains why we humans yearn for a deep, intimate experience best characterized as a pervading, or "other," dimension of reality. In our day, persons throughout the world are seeking a way of life informed by awe-inspiring and fascinating mystery, awareness of transcendent consciousness, personal experience of God and salvation. Today we witness a search for spiritual revelation, illumination, and insight. We yearn for the ability to live fully in harmony with self, otherselves, the natural world, and with the ground of our being. Wherever we look, we discover persons on a journey toward a consciousness in which subjective, depth experiences are as important as objective, empirically measurable, rational explanations.

Sacred and secular elements always coexist in every religious tradition, yet one or the other dominates at any given period in history. We believe we are emerging from an era in which the secular has dominated. Today we witness a swing of the pendulum and a return of the sacred, or the spiritual. The issue is how we will respond. Any legitimate response, we contend, will be open to other cultures and religions. By immersing ourselves experientially and reflectively in the practice and thought of the great religions of the East as well as the Eastern Christian spiritual heritage we can reassert the spirituality of our Western tradition and express our faith anew in a post-secular age.

Our personal commitment is to a spiritual life that integrates the eschatological and the historical so that our passion for personal experience and fulfillment is not estranged from a passion for social justice and human dignity for all. Our ideal is a spirituality that does not become exclusively a return to the inner world of religious experience. We believe a spirituality for our day needs to stress the incomprehensibility of God and therefore the provisional, tentative character of all theological statements; the corporate, personal, and cosmic aspects of life; an openness to insights from other persons' faith and of secular thought; the affirmation of both continuities and discontinuities in human experience; and a commitment to both the intellectual and intuitive modes of consciousness.

However, we are convinced that we Christians who have been socialized in Western culture need more than anything else to learn from non-Christians socialized in Eastern culture. Indeed, the age of the influence of Asian religions is already upon us. Just as there was once a Hellenized Christianity, with its many stages, so there is now the strong probability of an Oriental Christianity. In this process, the influence of Buddhism will probably be especially strong. And since we live in a connected world, Buddhism also will come under the spell of Christianity.

The East and the West present us with two different experiences, rooted in cultures and histories worlds apart. Still the worlds of oriental and occidental religion are not two worlds but one, one world with two perspectives, two perspectives dependent on each other. Increasingly we find that our many diversities come together—that behind the particulars and singularities there is a unity. We live in a "joined together" world, no longer segmented by physical barriers and less and less dominated by provincial ways. Now that the unity of humanity is within our purview, we are responsible for bringing the whole world into our lives. As Teilhard de Chardin wrote, "The task before us now, if we would not perish, is to build the earth." In the realm of religion this means more than toleration; it means the opportunity to learn from each other and to cherish each other. It also means a willingness to understand that our Christian "specialness" is not unlike those uniquenesses proclaimed by other traditions, and that it should provide no grounds for triumphalism. We proclaim that the Word becomes *flesh;* Buddhists assert that the lotus, the supreme symbol for the Buddha, takes root and grows in the *mud.*

In recent times many Westerners have taken a "journey to the East," to borrow the title of a novel by Hermann Hesse. Many people have traveled in search of meaning to religions once thought to be unknowable and alien. Unable to find within contemporary expressions of Christianity that experience of God and salvation all humanity seeks, they have found it helpful to take a spiritual journey into the practice and thought of Eastern religion. Some have found what they sought there, others have not. At the same time Easterners are seeking insights from the West. So it is that Buddhists and Christians meet; Orthodox, Roman, and Protestant Christians unite. Religion is that which links together and gives sense to the estranged, contradictory experiences of life. Religion gives meaning to people in every age through the medium of culture—a peoples' learned, shared understandings and ways—even as it points toward the sacred or to a transcendence.

One of the limitations of living in the United States is that many people can live their lives without ever meeting a Buddhist, or a Hindu, or a Muslim. There are places in the United States where people have never personally met a Jew. Indeed, many Americans still live only in the context of the Protestant Christian denominations and sects.

Nevertheless, in these late years of the twentieth century, we are becoming aware that not everyone speaks English and that many people neither need nor wish to do so. More important we are becoming aware that for better or worse the United States is not solely a nation of Christians and that we will need to learn to live in the context of religious as well as cultural pluralism.

A new generation, confronted by the inadequacies of their inherited traditions, is turning to other traditions for insight and illumination. Increasingly they can find in our larger cities and universities persons of other faiths. Many are searching for experiences within traditions other than those known in their original families. While there are few conversions from one faith to another, persons' lives are being shaped by their interactions with intelligent, devout, and righteous persons of Buddhist, Muslim, Sufi, Jewish, and Hindu faiths.

Of course intellectuals have always been curious about other persons' understandings and ways. Courses in world religions have always attracted students. But typically these have been studied as religious systems. Recently, this approach has been challenged by the Harvard historian of religion, Wilfred Cantwell Smith. Smith has made the important point that you can know a good deal about the various religious systems and still not understand the people who are committed to them. Through the years Smith has sought to help persons understand Buddhists and not Buddhism, to help persons to perceive reality the way Buddhists perceive it, to move from the study of other people's sacred writings, rituals, customs, and beliefs, to experience the faith of others.

It is our inner faith and not our outer religious system that needs to be shared. Only then can we learn from each other and both expand and deepen our own faith. In an important and insightful essay entitled "Christian — Noun or Adjective?" Smith demonstrates how the questions "Are you a Christian?" and "Are you Christian?" are vastly different. The first question relates to membership and participation in a historical community with its scriptures, customs, and beliefs; the second to an understanding of the spiritual dimension of one's own life and of others' lives. Smith explains that while persons cannot say they are both a Christian and a Muslim, they can say "I am both Muslim (insofar as a Muslim is one who is obedient to God's will), and Christian." The nouns, he points out, estrange and keep us apart; the adjectives make possible interaction, understanding, and even unity. We share Smith's contentions and concerns.

We believe, therefore, that we need to recognize the transcendence in each others' spiritual aspirations and, through shared experience, deepen our own spiritual life. Knowing God and salvation are adjectival qualities of our shared human experiences. They are manners of living, of being human—alone and in community. We each need to enter the faith, the perception of others, and we need to experience reality in this way. By so doing our own faith is enhanced and enlivened, our own experiences broadened and deepened.

Religious diversity is a social historical fact. Not all people are Christians; indeed most are not. We believe isolationism is unreasonable. Christians cannot afford to ignore other religious traditions. Nor is proselytizing evangelism a proper stance for the church. Exclusivism is also unreasonable. We cannot assume that if one religion is true another is false. Ignorance, arrogance, and disdain are improper human responses to the faith of other persons. We need to seek mutual understanding and admit that we can gain valuable insights from each other. However, doing these things is difficult. An enormous cultural gap separates East and West. Eastern and Western religions are vastly different. But we have so much to learn from each other. This plea should not be construed as a defense of a lazy tolerance of religious pluralism, or as a misplaced relativism which leaves it to the individual to choose from a cafeteria of varied options. Nor are we suggesting a common world religion. But we are advocating a Christian religion that is less parochial and more actively receptive to the total religious heritage of humanity.

The issue we face is learning to live together in mutual respect, trust, and loyalty. If we are to live together and learn from each other, we will need a deeper sense of our identity in a tradition as well as a greater sense of openness to each other. We need to arrive at a place where we can appreciate another's faith and life without losing allegiance to our own.

If we are engaged in the wider meaning of religion, we can no longer be content with the cerebral and often superficial spirituality that characterizes much of Western theology and life. Religious education in our day has failed to take seriously the spiritual dimension of life and the place of feelings and emotions. Contemporary Christian theologians have generally found it difficult to understand the place and influence of the unconscious depths.

So a new, but also old, meaning of religion has captivated us. In looking for a wider perspective that will allow us to grasp the possibilities of our world, in our need for and attachment to life-explaining and life-giving symbols, and in our quest for a new responsiveness, we are crossing religious boundaries and journeying to other traditions. This book will share our attraction to Eastern religion as Christians.

East and West. We are what we are and, no matter how influential the journey, no matter how great the enlargement of our understanding about religion, we remain Western and Christian. We advocate a chance to look and compare and learn. But we are claimed by and we are always reappropriating Christian understandings and ways.

In the West, we have so often been told that one particular way contains the truth in religion. As a result, we have been sold into doctrinal slavery. In a new time when exclusive competing faiths make no sense—and offer little hope for understanding, let alone compassion—we suggest that all religious doctrines be thought of as metaphors of universal truth. Let us not abandon the sharpness and helpfulness of our particular metaphors but realize that they point to something larger, something inclusive and elemental.

Our lives can have many facets, and multiple sources are available to use in our quest for value and understanding. We can only define people adequately by describing what they *aim* at being. What we have in common is a journey in search of the spiritual life, through various ways of knowing: a journey with beginnings and endings, alone and together, toward salvation. And so the content of this book.

In the chapters which follow, John Eusden will share a personal experience of a teaching or a practice from an Eastern tradition. The recounting will include a commentary on the experience and the practical issues it raises for our lives as Christians in the West. John Westerhoff will respond from his personal experience and reflect from the perspective of the Christian tradition. Throughout, we are concerned about the practical implications for church life and religious education. In the final chapter, we will again combine our insights on the meaning of the spiritual life.

CHAPTER TWO

The Real
Spiritual/Material

JOHN EUSDEN

During a January winter study period at Williams College, I was a co-teacher of an intensive course on *aikido*, a Japanese martial art. *Aikido* belongs to a whole family of Japanese physical arts, such as *karate, judo, kendo,* swordsmanship, and *kyudo,* archery. *Aikido* has nothing to do with breaking boards or throwing people around the room or through windows. The three Japanese characters standing for *aikido* are *ai,* together, *ki,* energy (or perhaps nature), and *do,* way or technique. The term means the "way of acting together with energy or nature."

Participating in the winter study course marked a return to the practice of *aikido.* My first work in *aikido* occurred during several teaching and research trips to Japan. This winter study period I was joined by two of my former students who have gone on to become black belt instructors in the art—Gordon and Anne Forrestel Greene. They, too, have spent time studying in Japan. Their proficiency and understanding were remarkable; they were the principal teachers in the course.

We gathered every weekday morning at 7:50 to do *zazen,* meditation, before practicing. Afternoons and evenings were spent in reading, discussion, and, occasionally, more practice. We joined together in weekend retreats. The program was unrelenting—it was also illuminating and unforgettable for teachers and students.

Aikido has its origins in the centuries-old tradition of the Japanese martial arts. It is known as a type of *budo,* or "the way of the warrior." It is truly a discipline, requiring great practice and dedication. It has a strong connection with Zen, but it has also been influenced by other Japanese religions and philosophies. *Aikido,* in its present form, is relatively new in the martial arts world. Its founder in the early part of this century was Morihei Ueshiba, an accomplished swordsman, a *jujitsu* specialist, and a wrestler. Ueshiba *sensei* moved away from the competitive and violent aspects of the martial arts. He changed the whole meaning of *budo* in Japan. Ueshiba *sensei* stressed that winning at someone else's expense is not winning at all. He even went so far as to say that *budo*—the way of the true warrior, as he defined it—was not based on struggle and power, but on love. *O sensei* stated, "It is the way of *budo* to make the heart of the universe our own, and perform our mission of loving and protecting all beings . . . the techniques of *budo* are only a means to that end." A practitioner does not "play" *aikido.* It is not a sport. It sponsors no competition and no points are scored. Therefore, there is no such thing as winning or losing in its practice. The only winning is over one's own aggressive tendencies and over one's own ego. Known superficially as a way of self-defense, it is much more a point of view and practice dealing with the self, others, and the world. Its stress is on harmony and movement. One's partner is never an opponent, but rather a collaborator and a co-seeker; partners bow to each other, recognizing and honoring a shared spirit. In good *aikido* technique, it is said that "two people are making one motion." *Aikido* is also described as "the art of moving Zen."

The meanings of *aikido* are many. It is to be an egoless discipline; its practice is to result in "centered wholeness." But perhaps its primary teaching deals with *ki,* or energy. *Ki* is the Japanese word for the Chinese parent word, *ch'i,* meaning matter and substance as well as energy. In *aikido,* one is conscious of letting energy flow forth from oneself to the partner and one is conscious of energy entering oneself from the partner. More important, the *ki* that one discovers in practicing *aikido* is all around one. When one rolls after being thrown, one uses the *ki* of the throw, the *ki* of one's own motion of "folding," the *ki* of gravity, and the *ki* of "pushing up power" as one rises to one's feet. All the parts of *ki* come together and one rolls with one motion, sustained more by the energy outside oneself than the energy inside. The analogy of ocean and waves is often used. As certain techniques are learned, one feels as if one were a separate entity like a wave; but one moves from that to feel, though still a wave, that one is, more essentially, part of the ocean. Both partners are aware of participating in a wide, surrounding field of energy—not divided into techniques, movements, or lessons.

Carl Jung in his study of the Chinese *I Ching, The Book of Changes,* speaks of the principle known as synchronicity, an acausal connecting principle, diametrically opposed to that of casuality. We do not cause energy. We tie in with it and become partners with it. Synchronicity stresses coincidence; it asserts that the meaning of events in space and time lies in a peculiar interdependence of objective events and the subjective state of the observer or actor. At certain moments in practice and discipline we are connected with something beyond ourselves which we do not cause. We intersect with an embracing power always present.

The Zen point of view which informs so much of *aikido* states that "Mind, having no fixed abode, should flow forth." We flow forth and connect. We are open and reality flows back into us, allowing us to understand and to perform techniques and ways. The word in Japanese for the ultimate "way" is *michi.* The word has the meaning of "abounding." The "way" of matter and energy is known

to us any time, anywhere, but most likely in our times of
practice and discipline. A Japanese *haiku* speaks of the
aboundingness of the ultimate "way" of energy and matter:

> A cool breeze
> Takes up abode
> Even in a single blade of grass.

A Zen master, poetically describing the Zen life known in
practice and discipline such as *aikido*, says

> If I scoop the water, the moon is in my hands;
> If I pluck a flower, fragrant is my robe.

In the practice of *aikido*, one is urged by a teacher to
develop the state of *mushin*, no mind. *Aikido's* movements
are soft, unforced, natural, flowing, spontaneous. These
yin qualities lead practitioners to become porous and receptive in their discipline, making it possible for energy
to enter and allowing them to return energy to others and
to the world. *Aikido* students abandon the yang stress on
violence, strength, abruptness, and domination as they
attempt to practice *mushin*. "Don't get in the way," teachers say, of the cosmic energy. It is unteachable in words
and it is a mystery, but it is there. Do not obstruct it.

In *aikido* there can be no dichotomy between spirit and
material, mind and body, self and others, personal energy
and cosmic energy. There is a famous Chinese story in
which a neophyte asked a master, "What is the one word
of reality?" The master answered, "You make it two." Everything we do, teaches *aikido*, is a part of and not separated from a single reality. A Buddhist teacher once
remarked, "I spend all day telling people what the *dharma*
(reality or teaching) is, but learners seem not at all to pay
any attention to my talk. How many thousand times they
tread on it under their very feet; and yet it is an utter
darkness to them."

To understand this lack of division and dichotomy, to

see things as ultimately connected, we need a new release of yin energy. The intuition's "quantum leap," immediacy, and openness to the feminine way stressed by *aikido* are part of the yin qualities needed so desperately in our time.

To do all this we must be mindful of what our body can teach us about breaking down dichotomies and divisions. In *aikido* we discover we are able to make connections and do things which were never before dreamed possible. I wondered if I would ever learn how to do a forward roll, fearful of hurting my back or shoulder. It was only when I discovered that arm, upper back, lower back, thigh, and knee were all involved and connected in the movement that I was able to do a beginning roll.

Aikido warm-up exercises give me a sense of reality beyond myself. Wrist rolls done in front of the face—revolving them rapidly as if they were on universal joints—and then shaking wrists and hands down at the sides open me physically to something extensive and encompassing. The tingling of wrists, hands, and forearms—those areas of the body containing so many crucial acupuncture points—awaken me and make me ready to enter into a larger field of energy. The spiritual becomes possible because of the physical.

The Reformed tradition was fond of speaking of "Jehovah" as a proper name for God. Reformed theologians believed that this term was taken from the root meaning of "he was"—or *fuit* in the technical theological language of the time. It meant that God is conceived as a symbol of the highest being and substance, who was and is and will be ever present to all people. We need to connect with this high being and substance and let this reality become a part of ourselves and ourselves a part of it. We need to cease our dichotomous existence, stop seeing things by reflection in a mirror; we need to see and recognize the wholeness of reality, as St. Paul says, "face to face."

One *aikido* teacher speaks of a supreme quality which,

it is hoped, will be possessed by those who engage in this practice. The Japanese word is *makoto*. It is often associated with honesty, but it means much more. *Makoto* is total sincerity, genuineness, the ability to seek after that which is true, real, and lasting. Ultimately, *makoto* as a virtue calls us to do away with any divisions—the inside and the outside, the spiritual and the material, the mind and the body. The person who practices *makoto* strives to become transparent, to become a vehicle for the "heart of the mater," which is what the Japanese word emphasizes.

To live in *makoto* is to practice connection and unity.

JOHN WESTERHOFF

Five years ago I made a retreat. It was my first experience of extended solitude and silence, without morning coffee, afternoon cocktail, or ever-present pipe; in their place was one small meal of bread, fruit, and cheese eaten in solitude and silence. Within the context of days devoid of conversation, books, and the stimuli of our culture's accepted drugs, I experienced a touch of wholeness and well-being unknown to me before.

Most important, however, three days alone provided me with a new experience of my body. After only a day, I found that I had ordered my time: rest and exercise, meditation and reflection, prayer and work. I further discovered that I had become attentive to my breathing and to each part of my body. Every bite of food was carefully chewed, savored, and swallowed; every inch of skin came to life as I patiently and attentively showered. My life, which I had unconsciously separated into a body, a mind, and a soul became whole and holy.

I returned to the "real world" and soon forgot these new awarenesses, though other experiences have caused me to reflect again on the significance of that retreat. I have observed the attraction of particular ritual actions. In a historically Protestant divinity school my students were being drawn to the imposition of ashes on Ash Wednesday, fasting on Fridays in Lent, foot-washing at the Maundy Thursday liturgy, the Stations of the Cross on Good Friday, being anointed with oil at public services of healing, the embrace at the Kiss of Peace, and the sharing of bread and wine at a daily Eucharist. I further became aware of exceptional interest in my course on the religious affections, the arts, and education; more significant was the overwhelming interest in dance by those who elected this course. Over and over again, my students expressed their awareness that the more attention they paid to their bodies and the senses, the more their spiritual life was enhanced and enlivened.

True, but strange. The popular piety in the United States is founded upon a dualism of body and spirit and a consequent separation of the sacred and secular, the spiritual and material, piety and politics. The repression of evil bodies, salvation of individual sinful souls, and the soul's passage to eternal bliss in another ultimately more real world summarizes the world view of our dominant religious tradition. It would seem that neither the religious nor secular culture in which most people have been socialized encourages an integrated, holistic understanding of human life.

Perhaps an acknowledgment of this unquestioned world view may help to explain some of our strange and conflicting human behaviors. It appears that the more we learn about the dangers to our health of smoking, the more we smoke; the more we learn about the dangers of alcoholism, the more we drink. In a nation blessed with an abundance of nutritional food and leisure time for exercise, we have a dominance of overweight, out-of-condition people. At the same time, while church attendance decreases, the health food industry, cosmetic business, and health spas increase. For every person with a can of beer in one hand and either a cigarette or junk food in the other watching grown people, professional athletes, mutilating their bodies, another is on a diet, jogging, and saving money for a face-lift.

There are some who take drugs to free themselves from their bodies, while others pray for the day when they will be released from their bodies to dwell in Heaven. There are members of every college class, typically known as "jocks," who spend hours developing the "body beautiful" while ignoring the library and the chapel. Others, identified as "eggheads," spend night and day exercising their minds and as little time as possible on physical activity or prayer. And still others, "the God squad," spend hours in prayer and Bible reading, but refuse to use their intellects to understand it or their bodies to act politically on its message. Some more seriously study one social issue after another, but rarely act; others become involved in every cause but rarely engage in serious reflection on their actions; still others say prayers, but rarely act or reflect.

This list of contrasting, conflicting behaviors could be expanded, but the point is that we humans act as if there were some natural separation between our bodies, minds, and souls, as well as different values to their individual importance. I must admit that I tend to live this way even though I am aware that doing so does not produce the wholeness or holiness for which I long. True, I don't smoke cigarettes, but I still chew on my pipe; I gave up the evening cocktail, but I still consume four or more cups of coffee a day; I diet, swim, play tennis, and sun in the summer, but in the winter I live on rich foods, gain weight, and limit my exercise to climbing the stairs from my office to our library and chapel. It isn't that I deny the importance of my body. I make sure that I have a yearly physical; I have memorized a host of diet plans; I admire attractive clothing, and I spend my share on cosmetics. It is just that for more than forty-five years, I have acted as if my body were somehow added to who I really am; I have thought of myself as *having a body*, rather than *being* a body.

What is the relationship between the body and the soul, the seen and the unseen, the material and the spiritual? What is real? These are not new or simple questions. Numerous, varied answers have been presented and defended throughout human history. There have been those who have believed in the existence of two primordial, separate, and mutually opposed principles, the material and the spiritual. There have been others who have believed in the existence of a single principle, which some said was material and others, spiritual. And there have been still others who have believed in a single unitary principle with two dimensions, one material and one spiritual.

Such complex philosophical formulations and discussions might appear esoteric and irrelevant except that they become manifest in our lives. Consider, for example, the difference in the behaviors of those who concern themselves only with saving individual souls for life in another world and those who concern themselves only with political, economic, and social life in this world. Or consider the disintegrated lives of those who vacillate between concern for the sacred and the secular, church and world, piety and politics, contemplation and action, as if they had no relationship to each other.

Many of the Christians I meet in local churches live as if they have bodies and souls. With the Creed, they may make an intellectual assertion concerning belief in the resurrection of the body, but they live by assumptions related to a belief in the immortality of the soul. I remember the furor caused by Oscar Cullman in 1955 when he delivered the Ingersoll Lecture at Harvard, "The Immortality of the Soul or Resurrection of the Body." Cullman contended that behind all Western speculation about a life-after-death lie two conflicting traditions. The ancient Greeks talked of "the immortality of the soul" and the Hebrews of "the resurrection of the body." Some assume

that the belief in immortality is simply a source of consola-
tion and an affirmation of the sacredness and absolute
value of the individual. But we cannot ignore the fact that
this belief has functioned as a defense for ignoring, down-
grading, or even despising all things temporal from the
human body to the body politic. Some assume that belief
in resurrection is used to provide an assurance of eternal
life. But we need to acknowledge that this belief has provided support for engaging in action for a new political
economic age of peace and justice. It is no wonder, then,
that the Second Vatican Council in its attempt to make
Christian faith relevant to human individual and social
life made the point that it is "not permissible to despise
bodily life." Nor is it coincidental that this same Council
reaffirmed the significance of both the sacraments and
social action on behalf of what the Jews call *shalom*—justice and peace.

In the Christian tradition, death is not natural or willed
by God. According to the Genesis myth, death came into
the world by human sin, hence the story of redemption by
the God who is life and the creator of life. For the Christian, every healing is a sign that the broken condition of
humanity has been redeemed. Every healing is a partial
resurrection, a partial victory over death by which the
anticipation of the body's resurrection becomes partially
visible in the earthly bodily life. While some Greeks as-
sumed that the body was evil and ordained to destruction,
Christian tradition has affirmed that the body is good and
intended for life. Thus, we need to take our bodies seriously.

The Hebrew understanding of life excludes a dualism
of body and soul. God is the creator of the body. It is good.
God gave that body life or soul. And God breathed God's
spirit into the body/soul thereby creating human life. We
humans share with all creation body/soul and we share
with God God's Spirit. As such we are an integrated whole.
The body is not the soul's prison; it is the temple, the
eternal dwelling place, of the Holy Spirit.

When we forsake our Jewish roots, we misunderstand the Christian tradition. Christian faith knows no separation of body and soul or, more precisely, of the inner and outer person. The inner person has no existence without the outer; it requires a body. And the outer person has no existence without the inner. Our Christian affirmation of the incarnation and the resurrection of the body belong together. Human life requires the incarnation and eternal life requires bodily resurrection.

When the Christian tradition speaks of "flesh" and "spirit" it is not talking about body and soul. "Flesh" refers to the power of sin and death which encompasses both body and soul, the inner and outer person. "Spirit" refers to the creative power of God; it encompasses body and soul. We are human insofar as we acknowledge and live in the spirit of God which is with us and within us. The "flesh" is our estrangement from God and the denial of our true human condition. Through the act of God in Jesus Christ, Christians believe that our essential human nature has been reestablished. That is, all humanity has been returned to its original, intended condition. Spiritual health is not a release from bodily life, but bodily life set free to live in the Spirit and to be truly human in relationship to God, self, neighbor, and nature—now and forever.

Paul's contrast of "flesh" and "spirit" was not a division between material and spiritual reality or between body and soul. William Barclay, in his translation of Romans 8:23, makes that quite clear: "We, too, even though we have received in the spirit a foretaste of what the new life will be, groan inwardly as we wait longingly for God to complete his adoption of us so that we will be emancipated from sin, body and soul."

The "flesh" in the Christian tradition refers to mundane life and worldly conformism, not to bodily life. To live in the flesh is to live a life that denies our bodies and others' bodies; it is a life of oppression, greed, injustice, prejudice, lust, avarice, and gluttony. The "flesh" is a false self. The real self is a unified body and spirit. Just as the body and spirit are dimensions of a unified life, so the material and the spiritual are dimensions of a single unified reality. The integration of these dimensions of reality results in harmony, wholeness, and health.

As the French philosopher, Merleau-Ponty, put it, "The body is not an object that can be taken apart, examined, and put together again. Its unity is always implicit and confused." We are our bodies and we cannot separate ourselves from our bodies. Spiritual health will elude us as long as we see the body as evil, sex as dirty, and carnal knowledge as pornographic. We need to learn to experience the integration of our bodies and spirits; we need to encourage an incarnate life-style infused with sensual and kinesthetic awareness. We need to take the physical needs and bodily existence of ourselves and others seriously.

A sacramental view of life, so alien to many, is founded upon an incarnational theology that unites the material and the spiritual dimensions of reality. In the Episcopal church's litany of healing we see an example of this understanding. It reads:

> God the Father, your will for all people is health and salvation.

> God the Son, you came that we might have life and have it more abundantly.

> God the Holy Spirit, you make our bodies the temple of your presence.

> Lord, grant your healing grace to all who are sick, injured or disabled that they may be made whole.

> Grant to all who seek your guidance and to all who are lonely, anxious, or despondent a knowledge of your will and an awareness of your presence.

Mend broken relationships and restore those in emotional distress to soundness of mind and serenity of spirit.

Grant to the dying peace and a holy death and uphold by the grace and consultation of your Holy Spirit those who are bereaved.

Restore to wholeness whatever is broken by human sin in our lives, in our nation and in the world.

Then the priest lays hands on each person and, having dipped a thumb in the holy oil, makes the sign of the cross on their forehead and says:

"*N*, I lay my hands upon you and anoint you with oil in the name of the Father and of the Son and of the Holy Spirit, beseeching our Lord Jesus Christ to sustain you with his presence, to drive away all sickness of the body and spirit, and to give you that victory of life and peace which will enable you to serve him both now and evermore. Amen.

Of course, the interplay between the mind and the body has a long history in the natural sciences. Physiologists have known that the emotions have an effect on the body. It has been established that certain mental conditions make persons susceptible to disease or result in what appears to be a disease. Psychosomatic medicine, holistic health care, and humanistic psychology have affirmed the unity of body and mind, but it is still easier for us to accept the idea that our mental or emotional health influences our physical health than it is to accept the contrary. It appears even more difficult to believe that our physical bodies affect our spiritual health.

Typically, physical education, like the arts, has been an extracurricular activity. As such, it has focused on competitive games which desensitize the body by focusing attention on the goal of winning. Many physical educators maintain that the purpose of physical exercise is to keep our body in shape; few suggest that physical education can be a means for spiritual awareness. Physicians tend to see health care as a means of helping us to feel better, more than a means for receiving spiritual energy. All too often minds rather than bodies are taught in church and seminary. But it is not enough to cultivate human functions in isolation from one another. The dimensions of reality and human life need to be related and integrated.

Some people fear that if they identify themselves with their bodies and the material world they will become alienated from the spirit of God, that they will be estranged from the sacred, the spiritual, or transcendent life. Perhaps we should fear the opposite. The sacred is always found in the mundane if it is found at all. The spiritual is discovered in the material, the soul in the body. Teilhard de Chardin contended that matter and spirit are not distinct entities in nature or in human experience. He further explained that salvation is not to be sought by abandoning the world, but in active participation with God in creation. In the *Divine Milieu*, he wrote, "In their struggle toward the mystical life, men have often succumbed to the illusion of cruelty contrasting soul and body as good and evil. But despite certain expressions of this tendency it has never had the church's approval."

Asceticism's historic relationship to austerity, fasting, abstinence, and mortification has been both misunderstood and, on occasion, misused. When they were misused they became ends; correctly they have always been means. The desert fathers fasted so that they might experience being fed by the Word of God; they were silent so they could listen to God; they limited their sleep so they could watch for the Lord. The vows of poverty, chastity, and obedience have also been misunderstood. At their best, they were not intended to produce a disengagement from the body or a denial of the material. Indeed, they were intended to affirm the significance of the body for spiritual health and to assert the essential relationship of the material and the spiritual. The vow of poverty was not a rejection of the world but rather an affirmation that all of creation was a gift of God, a grace to be acknowledged and held sacred. The vow of poverty, therefore, was intended to help persons realize that all material goods belonged to everyone and were not to be possessed by any one; the poverty vow was to help us become sensitive to the importance of the physical needs of people so that they might be served. The vow of chastity was not a denial of the body or the natural goodness of sexuality, but rather an affirmation of the sacredness of every body, of birth and the preservation of human bodily life. The vow of chastity was intended to affirm the human need for intimate, affectionate relationships with all persons, and to move us from restricted relationships and loyalties to the love of all humanity. The vow of chastity was to help us understand the holiness of sex and the sacredness of all bodily life. The vow of obedience was not intended to annihilate the will, but rather to affirm our human need to hear and do God's will; the vow of obedience was to help us discover that to be loyal to our true self is to be loyal to God.

The implications for learning and spiritual life should be obvious, though they will be difficult to realize for they go against the world view, the values, and the life-style of our culture. To come to an understanding of the material and the spiritual as two dimensions of reality, we will need to overcome the body-soul dualism and concentrate on the physical, bodily aspect of spiritual life.

In that regard we will need to take more seriously food and our eating habits. The importance of fasting in the church and the avoidance of fast foods will need to be advocated. To grow our own food, to prepare it with care, to eat it attentively, and to share it thankfully with others will need to become a way of life. We also need to pay attention to our hungers. Whenever we feel empty or anxious we also feel hungry. In need of acceptance and love, we stuff ourselves with rich food. As a result, we hurt our bodies and neglect the call of our spirits. Meditation on scripture, prayerful openness to God's grace, and humble participation in the Holy Eucharist can better meet our body's hunger pangs and our true human need.

We will need to learn to play and meet our body's need for exercise. We tend to burn ourselves out with work, indeed we turn play into work; worse, we are willing to watch others play expecting some sort of vicarious benefit. Good examples of noncompetitive exercise that permits us to integrate our thinking and feeling, our bodies and spirits are skiing, cycling, hiking, swimming, sailing, golf, archery, fishing, or jogging.

We will need to learn to listen to our bodies and respond. Whenever we have feelings we need to express, we are left with tensions in our body. Such feelings are a call to pray. One way of praying through our tensions, such as anger, is to take the person or situation we are angry at before God; act out our anger in our imaginations and be silent so that God can heal. We need to realize that our feelings of tiredness are calls to sleep and the world of dreams through which God calls us to new health and wholeness. We need to nurture our senses. We need to learn not only to see and listen, but to touch, taste, and smell. Our needs for a hug and human touching are a call to the community's Eucharist. More sensuous and kinesthetic liturgies and opportunities for retreat will help us to come in contact with the unity of our lives and experience God's gift of salvation. So will spiritual exercises such as fasting and meditative sport. Each of us, of course, will need to find our own way to live out poverty, chastity, and obedience so that while acknowledging and addressing our bodily needs we do not let them become all encompassing in our lives or deny them in the lives of others. The material and spiritual dimensions of reality and the body/soul-spiritual dimensions of human life can be integrated and made whole and holy, but if they are to be so integrated, we will all need to return to a much simpler way of life.

CHAPTER THREE

Awareness
Ways of Knowing

JOHN EUSDEN

It was June 1979. At the invitation of a friend and former student, I had traveled to Poona, India, to visit the *ashram*, religious community, of Bhagwan Sri Rajneesh. Hundreds of his followers live with him in the *ashram* or in the surrounding area of this old hill town. A daily migration of students and followers to the *ashram* begins at an early hour. Everyone wears orange! It is the "shocking orange of awareness and intensity," says Rajneesh, being a sign to the wearer and also to the outside world. The orange tide floods the gates of the *ashram*, flowing into Buddha Hall where Rajneesh's lecture begins at 7:45 A.M. I donned orange for a month and became part of the tide.

Bhagwan Sri Rajneesh was born in 1931 and became enlightened at the age of twenty-one. While no one can say what enlightenment meant for Rajneesh, at the very least it meant an ability to "see into himself deeply" and a resolve, similar to that of the Buddha, to follow the compassionate way of teaching. For nine years he served as a professor of philosophy at two Indian universities. His knowledge and expression of Western and Eastern philosophies and religions are immediately apparent in his daily discourses. He speaks movingly, as one might expect, of the Hinduism and Buddhism of his native India. Especially I think of his startling interpretation of Krishna, the central divine figure in the *Bhagavad-gita*, or *Song of God*, of Hinduism. Rajneesh is learned, provocative, and controversial. Criticism in India has since led him to reestablish his community in the United States.

As I became immersed in Rajneesh's comprehensive, seemingly eclectic approach, I asked myself, "Is there a principal strand in his teaching and in the life and spirit of the *ashram*?" Rajneesh would not like this question, for he believes that he represents no particular tradition. But I am a Western teacher who has been trained to classify, for better or for worse! I would say that his teachings are closely connected with the ancient religion and philosophy of China known as Taoism. Lao-tzu, the alleged author of the *Tao Te Ching—The Way and Its Power*, the most important Taoist text—is a favorite of Rajneesh. Once he remarked that he can lecture about Krishna, Buddha, Mohammed, Jesus, Bodhidharma (the first Zen patriarch), but that when he is speaking about Lao-tzu, "He and I are one." Rajneesh's own dwelling in the *ashram*—the place where he holds evening *darshan*, or small, intimate gatherings with followers—is called Lao-tzu House. Throughout all his lectures and writings, I catch the Taoist stress on change, aliveness, simplicity, unity, "doing by not doing," and the sense of the small revealing the large. Rajneesh offers his followers over and again a Taoist invitation: Practice the art of "deep let go" in order to be in harmony with yourself and with others. The nature of God is often described by Rajneesh in the language and symbols of Lao-tzu. In the *Tao Te Ching*, the Tao, or ultimate Way, is presented as "Something born before heaven and earth, in the silence and in the void . . . standing alone and unchanging, ever present and in motion." I see Rajneesh as a modern Taoist teacher. At least I know that as a teacher myself I have come to understand Taoism—and its influence on Zen—in a richer way for spending time with his books, listening to his lectures, and being in his presence.

But Rajneesh would say that various religious masters can be useful in the quest for self and community. He urges followers and listeners not to be sectarian or narrow, for all teachers have something to offer in our search. Rajneesh once remarked that great religious teachers are like the ocean—they all taste salty. At Poona, one confronts the serenity of the Buddha, the play of Krishna, the sharpness of the Zen stick, the water and wood of Tao, the parables of Jesus, the dancing of the Sufis.

I am impressed at the man's work and energy—lecturing seven days a week for two and a half hours each morning, offering individual and group *darshan* meetings every day, reading, writing, administering. Even if I were not attracted to him as a person, I stand in awe of his Puritan work ethic! A bubbling-over comic sense helps to sustain him—and sustain those who sit on a hard floor for lectures and participate in strenuous groups.

How can I describe the spirit of this community, this *ashram*? Upon entering, I immediately became aware of grace, joy, playfulness, and humor. I saw these qualities on people's faces, in their walk, and in the way they work. It appeared to be no ordinary humanity. People work seven days a week, but nobody looks at a clock; everyone seems to enjoy her or his work; it is a kind of creative play. People do not get tired; in fact, the deeper they participate in the strenuous life of the *ashram*, the more nourished they appear—full of energy and aliveness.

While in Poona, I did not become a disciple, or *sannyasin*, of Rajneesh and I did not seek a new name and blessing by opening myself to a spiritual and psychic link to the master. During my whole time in the *ashram*, I had to deal with my Protestant understanding of the "priesthood of all believers," for Rajneesh is called "Bhagwan," which means "Lord." I also had to deal with my Zen leanings toward a necessary separation of student and master—the process of looking by myself for my "true mind." Nor did

I wear a medallion with a picture of Rajneesh in its center around my neck, as does nearly every member of the *ashram*. And yet, I experienced Rajneesh as having the quality of a sage, of a saint, of a "high being." I see him as a person set apart, a teacher of a new consciousness. He became for me an illuminator of truth. Here within this caring community, I saw genuine, loving relationships and discovered a new spirit within myself.

I also learned that the discoveries in the *ashram* carry over into the lives of people after they return to the outside world. I think of a German dentist, a *sannyasin*, who had spent several long periods in the *ashram* interspersed by professional practice in his homeland. He spoke simply and movingly about his sense of liberation and about the vision of himself and his work which he gained in the *ashram*—insights which he had been able to carry back to his life of appointments, commuting, equipment buying, and community involvement. I wish I could have spent more time in Poona for work, meditation, the gaining of a sharpened consciousness about myself, others, and the world. I know that I am a questioner about Rajneesh and his community, but I am also one who has been moved and changed by time spent in his presence.

During my stay, I was especially interested in the many forms of meditation practiced in the *ashram*. At one point, I counted eight different kinds, offered either to beginning or continuing groups. The forms ranged from the classic, simple (yet difficult), emptying discipline of *zazen*, or Zen meditation, to contemporary techniques. One practice, introduced by Rajneesh, but with definite connections to Indian yogic disciplines, is called "dynamic meditation." It is done in a group upon arising in the morning, bleary-eyed and on an empty stomach. One does this exercise or meditation with eyes closed, or better yet, blindfolded. It has the following parts: (1) breathing—deep and fast, through the nose, using the whole body to

make inhalations and exhalations emphatic; (2) cathar-
sis—allowing your body to jump, move, dance as it wants;
(3) shouting—arms above the head, jumping up and down,
saying the *mantra* "Hoo, hoo, hoo," using the sound as a
"hammer below your navel"; (4) stopping—freezing in
whatever position you find yourself, trying to cease all
movement, within and without; and (5) celebrating—
dancing, moving, exulting, "being thankful to whatever
is in your self and is around you." This meditation exercise
is done to music—some very rhythmic, some melodic and
haunting. It concludes with the playing of a soft, flowing
sitar (an Indian stringed instrument) for the celebration
section.

The experience never failed to "clear me out"; it produced
within me a sense of my own expanding form; I experienced a glimpse into my true self as my mental chatter
stopped and I threw things off. During the day I was
conscious of the specialness of other persons, accepting
them and enjoying them, moving easily and with assurance among them. On some days, the impetus from dynamic meditation faded, but there was always the next
morning!

I have often wondered if there is a "first virtue" of the
spiritual life—by which I mean a strength (the original
meaning of virtue) or a perspective to be sought above all
others. The Greek philosophers taught the moral virtues
of courage, wisdom, temperance, and justice; Thomas Aqui-
nas and other Christian theologians spoke of the theological virtues: faith, hope, and love. St. Paul stated so
magnificently in 1 Corinthians 13 that "love is the greatest
of these." But, is there any quality of life which precedes
such moral and theological virtues? My experience in the
ashram in Poona leads me to say that it is the virtue of
awareness. While listening to Rajneesh's lectures, participating in the communal life, envisioning myself in new ways,
reflecting upon violence, and thinking about uses of ener-

gy in the world, I began to sense that awareness is the very starting point of our quest for spirituality.

The pervading spirit of the *ashram*, not just its programs, always focused on the first religious virtue of awareness. "To be aware," Rajneesh says, "is to do one thing at a time—with full watchfulness and consciousness." The Taoist-Zen stress on fully entering into the activity of the moment was lived out each day. I think how often I tend to do one thing while really planning and thinking about another, and thereby not being able to enter into either. As the Zen master Bokuju said, "I am simply eating and doing nothing else." We all need to listen, or dance, or work, or make love, or read, or sleep—and do nothing else—while we are doing that one thing. Rajneesh urged, in the spirit of the *Tao Te Ching* and of the Zen patriarchs, the living of each moment totally. It is only a "counsel of probability" within the *ashram*—let alone outside—but the teaching is that one should try to live "as if" one were totally involved in the moment. And then, perhaps, this kind of living becomes more and more possible. Since returning, I have found my "as if" moments transferrable to my ordinary pursuits so that I am increasingly aware of immersion in the activity of the moment.

Two of Rajneesh's books have helped me understand more fully this first virtue. The first is his discursive and anecdotal *Tao: The Pathless Path* (published in three volumes by the Rajneesh Foundation, Poona, India, in 1978). The second is his insightful commentary on the third Ch'an or Zen patriarch entitled *Neither This Nor That: Talks on the Sutras of Sosan*, published by the foundation in 1975.

Rajneesh urges people to look at themselves in a simple, direct, and honest way; he speaks of the integrated person as being one who has the qualities of the Taoist "uncarved block," i.e., who is "as she is," unadorned, solid, ready. "I am not a Messiah and I am not a missionary. And I am not here to establish a church or to give a doctrine to the world

. . . . My effort is totally different: a new consciousness, not a new religion; a new consciousness, not a new doctrine. Enough of doctrines and enough of religions. . . ." People need a new consciousness. Awareness or the "new consciousness" has no easy definition, but clearly it encompasses intuition and an open, responsive way.

The world of nature exemplifies this sense of awareness and indeed can be a teacher for all of us. Deer hunters know that when a kill has been made in a certain area, other deer immediately begin to leave, even though they have not seen their stricken fellow creature or heard a shot. They sense that violence has occurred and they move out. Rajneesh tells of experiments conducted on trees in India. The flow of sap quickens and tremors increase in certain species of trees when a woodcutter approaches, even before the axe is swung or the saw is started. A response to destruction is being made by a living organism.

Being aware often means just watching. When we are angry, we should not suppress our ire and hostility—Freud would agree with that—nor should we blatantly vent our feelings. While the human-potential movement often encourages its followers to blurt out their anger—to approach alleged wrongdoers and ask them to "accept my anger toward you"—Rajneesh urges his hearers to "watch" their anger. Monitor it. Do not hide it and do not let it burst forth. Watch it and see what it tells you about yourself. The anger will come and go; watch its rise and its fall. Be aware of what you learn about yourself in the watching—perhaps a new consciousness of yourself will emerge and a new way of understanding the reactions of others to yourself.

Work being done by field biologists has helped me to learn more from the world of nature. Those who work closely and scientifically with birds and animals find that their subjects have much to teach us about awareness. Dr. Holly Nichol, an ornithologist, is concerned with the preservation of the imperial parrot in the West Indies. She is intrigued with the calls and the singing of the parrots, as well as with their eating, mating, and nesting habits. On one of her field trips, a reporter asked her, "What are they saying?" She listened and then said, "They're saying, 'Here we are! This is our tree! This is our territory! Aren't we happy? It's a beautiful day!' " The parrots sing on for hours in the wilds of Dominica—until the dark shadows of the mountain climb high onto the steep slope—and Dr. Nichol studies and makes scientific notes, but she is aware of what is going on with her subjects. She senses the sanguine, positive, joyful character of their expression.

How easy it is to be unmindful of this first virtue! We allow barricades to be built around us—we encourage their erection and participate in their construction. We have been taught that daydreaming is an evil. We do not give ourselves the freedom to live, even for moments, in our fantasies. But daydreams and fantasies tell us much about our needs and our aspirations. The right kind of immersion can help us to perform, act responsively, and create in the real world. Also, we concentrate so much on our own egos and live so competitively that we are not truly aware of others; we do not listen to them and take in what is happening in the whole range of interaction. We are not aware in our selfish materialistic culture about what is happening to the world at large. Despite protestations and warnings, we are unaware that our forests and trees are not simply diminishing, but vanishing. The earth is losing forestland at the rate of 150 acres every minute. In another half century, there will be no point in speaking about forest ecology. Nor are we really aware of where our arms race is leading us. It is estimated that by the year 2000 as many as a hundred nations will know how to acquire, or actually be producing, nuclear weapons. Are we truly aware how close we are to global destruction in the development of our self-defense and "preventive weapons"?

Now I am back in the West, as they say in Poona. I had a taste of the first virtue and it remains with me as I move in the home circles of marriage, family, work, research, and play. I am more aware of being a Taoist uncarved block, trying to see myself as I am, uniquely myself, full of my own potential and energy. The time with Rajneesh helped me to understand the importance of "watching," observing my real needs and hopes. I would like to think that I have become more responsive to others, more sensitive. At the very least I have learned different ways of knowing. I began to trust my body and my feelings as well as my mind and my reason.

We Christians need this first virtue. Somehow it is overlooked in our practice, our teaching, our liturgy, and our understanding of the spiritual life. As I participated in Sufi and other forms of dancing each day at the *ashram*, I sensed we need more movement and celebration. Arthur Darby Nock, a college teacher of mine, once said in a course on early Christianity, "Religion is not believed, but danced." We need to know that awareness can lead us to restriction and concentration, such as a visual meditation on the cross, and also to expansion and widening, such as rejoicing in the limitless meaning of providence.

Surely some of these qualities of awareness are present in our Judaeo-Christian tradition. They are found in the book of Job and the Psalms as seen in the abundant references to the meaning of God's creation and nature. The Bible calls us over and again to a meditative awareness—"Be still and know that I am God" (Ps. 46:10). In Isaiah 43, "The Lord, your Redeemer, the Holy One of Israel," says, "Behold I am doing a new thing; now it springs forth, do you not perceive it?" The Bible continually reminds us that we are unresponsive, sluggish of heart, and unseeing. Jesus commands us in the Sermon on the Mount to "Look at the birds of the air" and "Consider the lilies of the field, how they grow" (Mt. 6:26, 28). In the Garden of Gethsemane, Jesus urged his disciples to be awake and to watch. The disciples were urged by Jesus not to dream, not to sleep, not to drift away—just to be fully present, conscious of the intermingling of despair and glory. The disciples were not able to do this; Jesus came and "found them sleeping, for their eyes were very heavy; and they did not know what to answer him" (Mk. 14:40). We have so much in common with those sleeping disciples. How do we interpret the parables which relate to the secrets of the kingdom of God? They speak over and over again of the first virtue of awareness. "For to him who has will more be given, and he will have abundance; but from him who has not, even what he has will be taken away" (Mt. 13:12). Awareness leads to more awareness but for those whose ears are heavy of hearing and whose eyes are closed and for whom there is no understanding with the heart, there will be less and less. In the same spirit, the later tradition of Ephesians speaks, "Awake, O sleeper, and arise from the dead" (Eph. 5:14).

In the unfolding history of the church we have the mystics, and St. Francis, and Jonathan Edwards. In our day, we need to recover and to live in *their* spirit of awareness as well as to learn from the East. I struggle to understand why this is so difficult for us and wonder what we might do to expand our ways of knowing so that awareness may become a virtue for modern Western Christians.

JOHN WESTERHOFF

It was a quiet day. I had no classes. The night before I had read Hermann Hesse's novel *Beneath The Wheel*. The story it tells, based in part on Hesse's own experience, constitutes an attack on educational systems that foster the intellect, purposefulness, and ambition to the detriment of emotion, instinct, and soul. I was struck by Hesse's moving tale, and troubled by how much my education had emphasized the intellect to the exclusion of intuition.

The date was October 28, the festival day of St. Simon and St. Jude, my baptismal day. A year before, friends had reminded me of the second of my patrons and reintroduced me to St. Jude, the saint of impossible causes, but it didn't mean very much. I wore the medal of St. Jude they had given me, but my upbringing had ignored saints, saints' days, and praying to saints. Having told some other friends about my saints, they had given me a reproduction of a fourteenth-century icon of St. Jude. Icons are portable images of religious subjects. Used in Orthodox churches to decorate the screen (iconostasis) dividing the nave (a symbol of the earthly, physical, material world) and the sanctuary (a symbol of the heavenly, spiritual world), icons point to their inseparability and symbolize the unity and reconciliation of the sacred and the secular.

In my icon Jude is clothed in martyr's red robes and is set on a gold background with a small boat in one corner. In one hand Jude holds a boat hook shaped as a cross, and in the other hand a fish. Icons are intended to foster intimacy. They are not to intrude on us, but they ask that we be patient and spend time gazing upon them in stillness and allow ourselves to be gazed upon by them. As such, icons are prayers and contemplation transformed into an art form. They are incarnational and therefore sacramental. They manifest God to us. They aid our devotion by mediating between two dimensions of reality and thereby make possible the graceful experience of salvation.

I placed the icon of St. Jude on a small table in front of me. I lit some incense and a candle. I put a recording of soft Eastern Orthodox chanting on the phonograph and sat cross-legged on my office floor meditating on my icon of St. Jude. I did not know what to expect, but it seemed, in the light of Hesse's novel, an appropriate way of celebrating my saint's day.

Time passed and I felt myself drifting into another state of consciousness. Before me was a vision of Jude. He spoke:

"John, we are friends, we share a vision. Do not lose heart. I am praying for you. Pray for me." Slowly Jude drifted back into the icon, the incense filled my head. I was on holy ground. I prayed that God would care for Jude in his continuing pilgrimage and that God would help me be faithful to the vision of God's kingdom we shared.

I have reflected on that experience many times since. Similar experiences have occurred. Praying to St. Jude, the Blessed Virgin Mary, and other saints has now become a part of my life, so have icons, incense, meditation, and contemplation. I have realized that if I can ask friends on earth to pray for me and I can pray for my friends, surely I can have prayerful communication with the saints. What else did I mean when I confessed belief in the holy catholic Church, the communion of saints, the resurrection of the body and the life everlasting. More important, I have come to realize that there is more than one way to know, that spiritual awareness and indeed life itself is greater than my intellectual use of reason alone.

While numerous writers for years have defended various ways to explain what most recently has been called the split-brain hypothesis, I am personally convinced that there are two distinctive ways of knowing: the intuitive and the intellectual. There are two identifiable modes of thinking: the affective and the cognitive. There are two dimensions of consciousness: the responsive and the active. The first is nonverbal and founded upon subjective experience; the second is verbal and founded upon objective reflection.

(1) The intuitive, affective, responsive way of knowing is characterized by surrender, mystery, imagination, surprise, and passion. It is at home with antistructure, ambiguity, chaos, and risk. It is a tacit way of knowing which is holistic, sensuous, mystical, and inner-directed— leading to awareness.

(2) The intellectual, cognitive, active way of knowing is characterized by prediction, logic and analysis, control

and disinterest. It is at home with structure, certainty, the familiar, and security. It is an explicit way of knowing which is linear, argumentative, rational, reflective, and other-directed—leading to comprehension.

While this intellectual way of knowing is at home in the world of time and history and is nurtured by language, science, and mathematics, the intuitive way of knowing is at home in the world of timelessness and eternity, and is nurtured by artistic endeavors and bodily emotional expression. While the rational way of knowing is expressed through signs, concepts, and reflective actions, the affective way of knowing is expressed through symbols, myths, and rituals.

Thomas Merton in his book, *Conjectures of a Guilty Bystander*, writes ". . . Today with a myriad of instruments we can explore things we never imagined. But we can no longer see directly what is right in front of us." The core of our spiritual problem lies in our Western tendency to externalize and objectify. Our talk and our thoughts about God do not bring us into a relationship with God. Theology as an objective rational science makes God a problem. For a long time the church has asked: "What has Athens (Greek culture) to do with Jerusalem (Jewish culture)?" Today the more important question is: "What has Zion (religious life) to do with Bohemia (artistic life)?" My answer is: *Everything*! The function of artistic expression is to illumine and draw us deeper into life's depths. The arts incarnate our experience of mystery, wonder, and awe and thereby aid us to encounter the holy or sacred. Without the arts we are cut off from most of the means by which we perceive life's ultimate meaning. As Rudolph Arnheim put it, "Art is society's most profound reminder that we humans cannot live by bread alone." The arts both express and nurture our intuitive, affective, responsive mode of consciousness. They remind us that faith precedes theology; that our knowledge of God is prior to our conceptualization of God. They help us understand that our sense of God's presence is an intuitive, affective experience. Meaning begins with the feelings and moves from feeling to intuition and on to thinking or rational analysis. "The symbol gives rise to the thought," wrote Ricoeur. Religious thought is grounded in religious experience. Our personal encounter with that ultimate mystery which is God is nurtured, expressed, and communicated through dance, painting, music, sculpture, poetry, and drama. Religious life and artistic life go hand-in-hand. While that is my conviction I am aware that many persons in the church may not agree or understand what I mean. We are, I suppose, our history. As I sit in my library-study at Duke surrounded by pieces of art created or given to me by students and listening to the university's classical music station, I remember vividly the days when this conviction began.

In the mid-1950s I was a student at Harvard Divinity School. Those were the days of my intellectual searching for truth. I was questioning whether it was possible to speak meaningfully of God. I had been educated in a secular-scientific world view. I accepted the assumption that the natural world works according to its own inherent logic; that social and personal life results from comprehensible, predictable cause and effect relationships. Having been introduced to religious pluralism and the truth claims of Jews, Buddhists, Moslems, and Hindus, I tended toward philosophical relativism and doctrinal skepticism. Still I nursed a longing for the sacred. A significant experience helped me in those days: I came to Paul Tillich, the theologian (who was one of my teachers), with a request for an intellectual response to one of my several areas of theological doubt; instead of answering me in kind, he turned on his record player so that I might hear the "Credo" from Bach's *B Minor Mass.* I will never forget that moment; the only answer the great theologian had for his students' intellectual search was the church singing its faith, singing "Credo"—"I give my love, my loyalty, my heart. . . ." Ever since those days, I have been convinced that the arts better than the sciences mediate, illumine, and express the spiritual dimensions of life. Religion is indeed danced before it is believed. Religious experience begins at the level of symbol, myth, and ritual, rather than signs, concepts, or reflective actions; religion begins with the affections—not intellectual conviction. All of life— indeed religion itself—is comprised of sacred and secular elements. The secular points to the surface of life—the objective dimensions of reality; the sacred points to the depths of life—the subjective dimensions of reality. Throughout history, one or the other has been dominant. When the secular dominates, science and philosophical- theological reflection assume greater significance; when the sacred dominates, the arts and affective, intuitive expe- rience assume greater significance. Both modes, of course, are important. That is what Julian of Norwich in the four- teenth century was trying to explain when she wrote, "Man endures in this life by three things, by which three God is honored and we are furthered, protected, and saved. The first is the use of man's natural reason. The second is the common teaching of the holy church. The third is the inward grace giving operation of the Holy Spirit. And these three are all from one God." Education according to Julian is an awareness of the process by which we experi- ence and make sense of ourselves and our world. The process, she contended, begins with religious experience and proceeds with an intuitive exploration of our affec- tions, informed by reason and illumined by our corporate memory. Today we are living through the death of the secular. We are witnessing the last gasp of speculative theology and meditative spirituality. A rebirth of the sa- cred surrounds us. A new affective theology and a contem- plative-active spirituality is emerging. As a result the science of theology and biblical criticism are being balanced by a concern for the religious affections. Once again, the arts and liturgy are emerging as the content and context for both religious experience and religious education. There are dangers, of course. But even as we strive to integrate the intuitive and the intellectual modes of consciousness, we need to acknowledge that the point of entry for meaningful religious life is the intuitive. We need, of course, to beware of an anti-intellectualism. We need to avoid a pietism which focuses exclusively on personal, individual, subjective emotion. As I have said, there are two ways of knowing, two modes of thinking, two dimensions of consciousness. One we know well—it is the foundation of our educational practice and the primary concern of parents and teachers in church and society: it is an intellectual way of thinking, an active mode of consciousness. The other way of knowing is intuitive, an affective way of thinking, a passive mode of consciousness. Not only is this latter way of thinking dominant in childhood, it is basic to all life and primary for all learning. Of course, it is the two together that make for maturity in human life.

Having lived in the South and made it my home, I have rediscovered the arts and the affections, but I also witnessed what can happen when they are distorted by an excessive concern for a right feeling and emotion. Balance is required if we are not to fall into the heresy of pietism. Indeed balance is required if we are not to fall into the heresy of rationalism. All too many people have been victimized by a false religion of subjective emotionalism devoid of both thinking and imagination. Nevertheless, intellectuals would do well to remember that in our scientific age we have by and large lost contact with the dimensions of reality that give rise to the religious. Lest you worry that the arts can lead us away from a faith that does justice, let me suggest that great art is prophetic as well as priestly, that it both brings us into contact with the holy and confronts us with a critical revelation on our common life. The artist further teaches us that we cannot live in our own private experience, but must in some way incarnate it or bring it into being. It was Picasso's *Guernica* and Rouault's *Ecco Homo* that first awoke in me a concern for peace and justice. My colleague in moral theology, Harmon Smith, shared with me a story of his visit to Dachau where amidst the horror of that place he sought out Pastor Reiger, the Lutheran pastor of the chapel, a one-time inmate at Dachau, and asked him how this could have happened in the land of Luther and of Bach. Pastor Reiger responded, "It is easy to understand, the church had become very practical and intellectual, it had forgotten the Bible teaching that without visions the people perish. Hitler knew that and gave our people a vision." Then he whispered in my colleague's ear, "Pastor Smith, never forget where there is no vision, there is no risk; where there is no risk, there is no witness; where there is no witness; there is no Gospel; where there is no Gospel, there is no hope." I can also recall Amos Wilder, before he wrote it in his book *Theopoetic*, saying that it is at the level of the imagination that the faithful issues of our world must first be mastered. It is in the imagination that culture and history are broken. We should remember, Wilder said, that human nature and human societies are more deeply motivated by images and visions than by ideas; by experiences more than by dogmas. In that regard, I recall Georges Florovsky, one of my teachers at Harvard, lecturing on Cyril of Jerusalem and John Chrysostom. He reminded us that the shaping of the affections and dispositions of the heart was a fundamental intention of their catechetical strategy. Cyril of Jerusalem, he commented, had a particular concern for the preparation of "the heart" and "the illumination of the spirit." John Chrysostom, he continued, emphasized the significance of the affections surrounding the sacramental rights and the importance of "passions" for baptismal candidates.

I recall Will Kennedy, when he was with the World Council of Churches, telling of the long lines of worshipers moving slowly through Trinity Cathedral in Zagorsk, Russia, past the tomb of the saint who founded the monastery, chanting continually, with the smell of incense strong and the rich silver and gold icons everywhere. "It appears," he commented, "that the formation of Christians occurs not by rational design and process but by total emersion in a community of faith worshiping God through all the senses."

Urban Holmes, with whom I wrote *Christian Believing*, explains in his seminal book *Ministry and Imagination*, that if we are to be open to the presence of God we have to live a life of imagination. If God is absent, it is because we have so little imagination. To imagine is to be human. To be human is to imagine God. None of this, of course, is new. From the beginning, the Christian community expressed its faith through the arts. From the Roman catacombs where Christians met secretly to the great medieval cathedrals we find artistic offerings to God. The musical, dramatic, and visual arts played a significant role in the church's life and worship just as they served as effective means for education and catechesis. During the ninth and tenth centuries the liturgy of the church became increasingly dramatic; symbolic gestures, dialogical responses, and antiphones interspersed with anthems and hymns transform the liturgy into a community drama and dance using all the senses for the worship of God and the nurture of humans. During the eleventh century the churches erected in their naves scenes to be used in the dramatization of the Christian story from creation to the last judgment. Through pantomime and tableaux, the Scriptures were brought to life. By the fifteenth century, the average person was heir to a vital musical, dramatic, and poetic tradition. In an age of relative illiteracy, the arts transmitted the Christian faith.

Throughout the Middle Ages and much of the Renaissance, Western art was explicitly Christian in content and style. However, the age of reason combined with the reformation and estranged the church and the arts. The artists sought liberation from the restraints of the church and the church turned its back on the artists. By the eighteenth century the divorce was all but complete. While society has never been without great religious art, their works typically have been restricted to galleries and museums. Today, church architecture is generally unimaginative. Few great paintings or pieces of sculpture adorn the church. Prints of sentimental pictures of Jesus and trivial pieces of music combine to further alienate the artist from the church. Drama is often restricted to the children's Christmas pageant, and dance is all but nonexistent. The verbal and the intellect dominate liturgy and education. It is because of our overreliance on reason and neglect of feelings that poet Denise Levertov suggests that poets today, in a peculiar way, are the believers and the theologians and preachers the skeptics.

Along with Rudolf Otto, I contend that what is most distinctive in religion cannot be put into words. This is the nonrational, that which is not capable of being conceptualized. The nonrational is a numinous experience, partly a feeling of dependent creatureliness and partly a consciousness of something outside us that is wholly other.

While Western Christianity has become highly rational, we must never forget that the essential core of religion is in danger of being lost under a cloud of rationalizing. At the core of religion is a nonrational element that cannot be conceptualized or put into words, though it can be communicated.

Religion belongs to the sphere of the unsayable, the absurd, the world of non-sense which, if it is to be put into words at all, must use metaphorical images, symbol words, or poetry. Religion is better sung than recited, better danced than believed, better painted than talked about. That is why religious education is dependent on the arts. That is why children—those who are dependent, nonrational, nonproductive beings—can have religious experience and, more importantly, can help adults, who have become independent, rational, and productive, to rediscover the holy. Only if the religious affections and the arts become basic to human life will persons acquire those perceptions and share those experiences which make it possible for us to be fully human in community. Only through the imagination will we gain those insights and understandings necessary for human survival. We have for too long neglected the development of our conscious and unconscious minds. We have limited our human capacities, we have neglected our deeper consciousness and estranged ourselves from our creative selves. Until we can restore the religious affection to this proper role in human life, we will remain captive to our conditioning and separated from meaningful relationships with God, self, neighbor, and nature. Human individual and corporate life is at stake in the estrangement of Zion and Bohemia. Their reunion may well be the greatest challenge facing religious education in our day.

CHAPTER FOUR

Actualization
Life in Wholeness

JOHN EUSDEN

Let me relate and reflect upon two experiences, one Zen and the other Taoist.

My friend and colleague Masao Abe asked me to join him and others for *zazen*, meditation, at Mioshin-ji, a major Zen temple compound in Kyoto, Japan. We met in the subtemple known as Reiun-in, "Spirit of Cloud Temple." I entered the gate of Reiun-in and walked along its paths, on the gravel and stepping stones, passing by some of its gardens. I took off my shoes just outside the *zendo*, or meditation hall. I walked across the firm, resilient floor mats, or *tatami*, to a set of cushions over which had been inscribed my name in Japanese *katakana*. It was cold during the winter of 1963–64 in the unheated *zendo* and I had not worn enough clothing. Somehow I lasted through the three sittings and *kinhin*, or walking and relaxing meditation, separating the *zazen* periods.

The "Spirit of Cloud Temple" meditation experience also lasted in me; it was the beginning of an ongoing practice and discipline. Later on a subsequent trip to Japan, I joined Reiun-in and was formally accepted into membership in a temple society dedicated to Zen meditation and discussion. Various retreats and *sesshin*, "times of collecting thoughts," in this country, often accompanied by students, have given me further insight into this central Zen practice. Now, *zazen* has become part of my spiritual way.

How could I teach Taoism to American students in a large standard course, using books, lectures, diagrams on the blackboard—and other necessary techniques? Normal teaching seemed so foreign to an ancient Chinese religion which states simply, "The Tao (or Way) that can be named is not the real Tao." Following the example of Lao-tzu and Chuang-tzu, alleged founders of Taoism, I urged my students to engage in the pratice of "Taoist walking." The practice became a regular component of the course—students were to reflect upon the exercise as part of a later term paper. I entered into the discipline also, sometimes in the company of students and sometimes by myself. The practice is based on ideas presented in the *Tao Te Ching, The Way and Its Power,* and in the *Chuang-tzu,* a book named after its presumed author. Among other things, a Taoist walker concentrates on the rhythm of her pace, the swing of her arms and legs; she engages in deep, natural breathing; she observes the surrounding natural world; and she is caught up in a process of "letting go," or emptying. Taoist walking, like *zazen,* has become part of my spiritual way.

Both of these practices have presented to me a sense of wholeness about my life.

Zazen is often thought to be an individual, isolated religious practice. But it is highly connective. One does *zazen* with other people; energy is shared; one senses a unity with the long history of Zen practitioners. One is very conscious of being joined to the floor—and horizontally with all those who have made it possible for one to engage now in this practice. Vertically, one is connected with the quest for an original self, cutting through misrepresentations and false fronts. A Zen teacher will often say, "Find your original face before your parents were born." Be connected with original being, or something that is one and uncaused. Don't be concerned with *maya*, the many, the multiple—there is no end to that search. The Zen sense of being connected with something elemental reminds me always of Jesus' saying, "Before Abraham was, I am." (John 8:58)

A person starts in the discipline by sitting in a firm, but relaxed posture—usually cross-legged with knees on the floor. A process of centering begins by concentrating on exhalations and then inhalations. One should let distractions go (so easily said!), as consciousness is transferred to the center of the body—"four fingers' width below the navel." One should try to be empty but awake, as Zen people say.

A Zen teacher has said that *zazen* is "just holding yourself steadily in front of the truth." It is a kind of subtle death in which one lets go in order to expand and take in—so that one may find relatedness and a sense of connection and no longer live in scatteredness and division. *Zazen* is a different kind of adventure! It is something that does not happen *in* the mind, but happens *to* the mind. The wholeness and centering that arise from the discipline do not take you away from the world but have the power of placing you very much in the middle of things—with 360° vision.

As for Taoist walking ... the historian George Trevelyan once observed, "I never knew a man to go for an honest day's walk for whatever distance, great or small ... and not have reward in the repossession of his soul." Many of us would share Trevelyan's feeling about the reconstitutive qualities of walking. But, like most religious disciplines, the spirit of walking is not easily achieved. Henry Thoreau once said, "I have met with but one or two persons in the course of my life who understood the art of walking, that is, of taking walks—who had a genius, so to speak, for sauntering: which word is beautifully derived from idle people who roved about the country in the

Middle Ages, and asked charity, under pretense of going 'a la Sainte Terre,' to the Holy Land, 'till the children exclaimed' There goes a 'Sainte-Terrer,' 'a saunterer, Holy-Lander.''

Lao-tzu's suggestions about walking are filled with the promise of wholeness. We must be conscious of the small—the particular leaf, the eddy in a stream, the subtle colors in pebbles. From these microcosms we proceed to observe and contemplate and so to grasp connections in a macrocosm. On the first half of a Taoist walk it is good to observe only the small—to really observe the myriad of things about you. In the second half, expand your gaze and your awareness to take in the whole horizon, the colors of the sky—matching or contrasting with those of the earth, the energy of your breathing participating in the energy of the wind. It is said of one Taoist sage that he could ride the wind. He was so in tune with the movement of air outside himself through the naturalness of his own breathing that he could identify with and go with the larger force. As a walker, he moved without effort—he floated with the forces around him.

The wholeness of this discipline is seen also in its understanding of communication among those engaging in a walk. On the first half, discussion of particular objects is engaged in—and the naturalness of humor and laughter is encouraged. But the second half is done in silence. Those in the practice learn that the wholeness of communication includes no talk as well as talk. Some things are to be said. Different things can be shared when people talk without words.

The words medicine and meditation come from the same root; they are both healing forces. Meditation is an inner healing force and medicine is a healing force from the outside. The principal stumbling block for most Westerners in the practice of *zazen* is the desire to achieve. It obstructs the healing force directly. One does *zazen* because it is a good thing in itself, not because it gets one somewhere. Moreover, desire produces the concept of duality wherein one is aware of the observer and the observed. There is separation at the very beginning when one "aims at something." Meditation becomes a means of "seeing" the truth about wholeness.

Taoist walking has many emphases similar to *zazen* in the quest for wholeness. It is less structured, more spontaneous, and subject to many more stimulations from the outside world. In this discipline, one is directed to practice *kensho*, or the art of seeing things as they are—the art of observing, appreciating, and accepting. I often think of the words of James Taylor's song "The Walking Man."

Keeping an eye on the Holy Land . . .
Leaves have gone a-turning,
Geese have gone to fly . . .
Walking man walks.
Every other man stops and talks, but the walking man walks;
Frost is on the pumpkin,
Hay is in the barn,
Happy has come around . . .
And the walking man walks . . .

Nonetheless, Taoist walking and *zazen* have their parallels. They stress connection, a gestalt, or a field of connected energy, and a spirit of the whole. As Willa Cather said in *My Antonia*, "That is happiness—to be dissolved in something great and complete." Chuang-tzu put it this way in a typical Taoist-Zen natural reference: "Fish forget themselves in water; people should forget themselves in Tao."

These Zen and Taoist practices have led me not only to a sense of interconnection with others and with aspects of nature, but also to a new sense of schedule and time. I have stopped wearing or carrying a watch for the last two years. I find that I am more connected with what is going on with others, with what is happening in the natural world about me—perhaps clued into a greater rhythm and sched-

ule than just my own. Furthermore, a more positive understanding of time has come to me; I try to live in time and
not just by time. It seems that I appreciate time and its
passage more, that I am less manipulative and controlling.
Certainly, there seems to be a diminution of the dualism
of time and me. Time is something that I contend with
less.

Zazen and Taoist walking can only be appreciated by
participation! But books help and let me suggest a few.
Two books on Taoism and Lao-tzu come to mind: Max
Kaltenmarck's *Lao-tzu* and Holmes Welch's *The Parting of
the Way*. The two most illuminating books I know in English on *zazen* are *Zen Mind, Beginner's Mind* by Shunryu
Suzuki and *Zen Comments on the Mumonkan* (a collection of
forty-eight Zen *koan* or puzzling, jolting questions used
during meditation), by Zenkei Shibayama.

It is said of Picasso's art that it made possible a "free
passage from feeling to meaning." So it is with both these
practices. We enter them with a feeling, an inclination, a
thirst having to do with something we sense lacking in
our lives. Certainly this is true of the place of silence in
each practice. We give in to this feeling and discover that
meaning emerges about wholeness. Of course, if silence
is so important, why do we talk about practices and write
books about them? Perhaps talking and writing are different
after one has had "the free passage." Basho, the Zen *haiku*
poet, once was asked why he continued to talk and yet still
spoke against talking. He said, "Others talk—I bloom."
Talking and articulation can be different after a grasping
of the whole; they just happen, almost without effort—
they become truly natural phenomena.

When we use all of our senses and modes of understanding, we are able to see things as they are. We are told that
Lao-tzu was once asked why he walked silently every
morning. He replied, "In order to see things directly." We
do see things directly when we engage in such disciplines

as these—things directly as they are and in connection with everything else in the cosmos.

It appears to me that these Zen and Taoist emphases on wholeness are not unconnected with our own tradition. How can one read the psalmists without being overawed by their sense of connection with all of creation and with the glories of the natural world? Or how can one read the prophets without the sense of being connected with injustice and suffering in the world? Jesus continually lives in the whole. This is so in regard to himself, to others, and to his understanding and use of time—the time now and the time to come.

JOHN WESTERHOFF

My first experience with the Benediction of the Blessed Sacrament came when I was traveling alone in Latin America. It was a Wednesday evening. As I wandered through the streets near my hotel, I heard the bell of an Anglican church summoning the people. I joined them. The first part of the liturgy with its collects and canticles, Psalms and Scripture readings was familiar; the second was not. I knelt in silence as the door of the tabernacle behind the altar was opened and a monstrance in the shape of a cross was removed and placed on the altar. It contained a consecrated Host. Amidst flickering candles, Eucharistic hymns and silence, I stared at the wafer that, at an earlier Mass, had become the Body of Christ. Then it happened. Jesus appeared to me. I was struck by the fact that this human Jesus had both masculine and feminine qualities, was my sister and my brother (as Julian of Norwich used to say), and was also the resurrected Christ. This Jesus touched me. A centeredness, a healing sense of wholeness and completeness of life engulfed me. Here in this strange environment I had met my Lord and received a sacramental blessing; I knew the meaning of grace in its fullness.

I had experienced the presence of Christ before at the

Eucharist, but it is easy to forget Jesus' promise to be with us always. The reserved sacrament has become for me a symbol of Christ's continuous living presence, transforming and molding my life day by day. I am aware how strange and difficult this might be for some to understand; it was a new experience for me.

In previous chapters, I tried to make two points. First, with Archbishop William Temple, I asserted that Christianity is avowedly materialistic. It is so because its faith is founded upon the conviction that the material world is God's vehicle for divine grace and truth. St. Thomas, recall, contended that when we look on creaturely beings within the world and consider them "in depth" our mind is carried beyond them to God. At the Benediction of the Blessed Sacrament this is expressed in St. Thomas' magnificent Eucharist hymn which speaks of the glory hidden "beneath these shadows" through "faith our outward sense befriending, makes the inward vision clear." Second, recall that after establishing the unity of the material and the spiritual, I defended an intuitive way of knowing and the imagination as a means of bringing us into contact with dimensions of reality otherwise unavailable to us. Perhaps that helps to explain my experience. Others have had similar experiences.

John MacQuarrie recounts his experience in *Paths in Spirituality*. The doors of the tabernacle were opened, the Host was exposed in a monstrance and sensed as two great hymns of St. Thomas were sung. Between the hymns was absolute silence. The environment enlivened his imagination. His mind was freed of all thought as he recounted his experience and I reflected on mine. I began to understand the character and power of contemplation. Most of the time, at worship, we talk, have our intellects enlivened and do things. I learned that it is important to also do nothing, to empty ourselves and let God come to us. In that moment of kneeling quietly in God's presence, I had experienced wholeness and holiness. It was beautifully expressed through the collect in which we prayed that we might so "venerate the sacred mysteries of your body and blood that we may ever perceive within ourselves the fruit of your redemption."

Following this quiet mood of contemplation, MacQuarrie explains that the priest took the monstrance and blessed the people. At the very heart of our moments of devotion, God takes the initiative and blesses us through Christ. We respond in praise and thanksgiving, ending with Psalm 117. For me the Benediction of the Blessed Sacrament has become an opportunity to perform an act of open waiting upon God, of permitting God to make Christ's presence known, of letting God speak to me that I might come to know who I am and experience the health and wholeness, the actualization of human life God wills for all humanity.

As I have talked with my students and others in the church, I have discovered that this experience of being and wholeness is rare. Most people, it seems, only experience themselves as torn and twisted, as being unable to do what they want and often doing what they do not want to do. Most people experience their human life as fragmented, distorted, broken. It's easy to have that sort of experience. Only the naive or the blind can be oblivious to the evil in the world, in the social organizations and institutions we have created, and indeed, in ourselves. Christianity has always rejected a naive optimism which denies cosmic, social, and personal evil. But what many have forgotten is that Christianity also has rejected a gloomy pessimism which sees human nature as totally depraved.

Without assuming that our human sinfulness is an illusion, we need to reassert the Christian tradition's affirmation that we humans are fundamentally good. While capable of terrible depravity, a basic goodness is still latent in human nature waiting to be freed. God created humankind good, and God has acted in Jesus Christ to free us to be what God intends.

Being is the basic category of human existence. Being in harmony with God, with our true self, with all other persons and with the natural world is what God intends; it is also what we humans long for and what God has made possible for us.

I remember once going on a retreat. I arrived physically, emotionally, and spiritually exhausted. I was estranged from those I love most, I had lost God and I didn't feel very good about myself. My spiritual director took one look at me and brought me a collection of children's fairy tales. She suggested I read them until I fell asleep and that we'd begin my retreat the next day.

I did just that. A common theme seemed to run through all the fairy tales she left me to read. The main character, who in reality is royalty, is raised as a nobody. Then when the child grows up, he or she, through a revelation, discovers his or her true identity. It is an experience of being born again, but it begins a long struggle with the forces of evil until in the end this person becomes who he or she really is, and lives in a state of total bliss and thereby brings to the whole realm wholeness and holiness of life.

I fell asleep and dreamed I was royalty; I could not earn it, it was a gift and I was called to acknowledge my true condition and be who I already was. I woke up rested and ready for my retreat. My problem was not that I thought too highly of myself but that I did not think highly enough of myself. The next day, my director told me to imagine a host of angels going before me proclaiming, "Make Way for the Image of God."

This faith is at odds, of course, with our culture. The supreme goal of our culture is to possess. Our worth is gauged by how much we have. Our society is centered around things. Fortune, fame, and power are dominant themes in our national life. We typically say that we have a mate, food, a job, a degree, a home, and even a problem. Rarely do we say, "I am happily married; I am blessed with a full table; I am a teacher; I earned a Ph.D.; I live in a beautiful home; or I am troubled." Still our Christian tradition reminds us that we are to be and not to have. It is because the society in which we live is devoted to acquisition and possession that we experience alienation rather than actualization.

Being, of course, implies a process of change and growth, it assumes becoming. We are and we are not yet. The kingdom of God has come and yet is coming. God has acted in Jesus Christ and made us new persons. Actualization is the process of becoming who we already are, namely whole, healthy, good people in community. As Alan Jones, a priest, friend, and spiritual guide, once said as he held up the bread at the Eucharist and quoted Augustine: "Be what you see. Receive who you are!"

Erich Fromm, in his book *To Have or To Be*, discusses our contemporary misuse of the words *active* and *passive*. Activity, he suggests we define as purposeful behavior that brings about some discernible effect; as such it refers only to behavior and ignores the person behind the behavior. It matters little, he explains, whether a person's activity results from an external force or an internal compulsion in which we are not so much the actor as the one who has been acted upon. Which is really productive passivity? That is why, he explains, we experience alienation in our lives. The experience of actualization results from our being truly active, or being the subject of our activity. This, he suggests, is at the center of contemplative life, life lived out of the center of our being.

That may help to explain why Thomas Merton who, in his last days as a hermit, physically as remote as anyone can be from people and society, was more in touch with the world and more truly present to the world than most of the rest of us. Aware of both the inward and outward crisis confronting humanity he advocated the need for a contemplative dimension to human life.

Our search for God lies in our being aware that we are possessed by God. We need to learn to rest in God, to listen in silence to the God who has already found us. Contemplation is our active effort to keep our hearts open so that God might enlighten us. Contemplation is the gift of awareness, awareness of our true selves, of God, of our community.

Contemplation helps to understand *kenosis* or self-emptying, an experience lost in our busy achievement-conscious culture. We need to learn the possibility of self-emptying that we might participate in the mind of Christ, which is the transformation of our consciousness or awareness that St. Paul spoke of when he wrote to the Philippians, "Let this mind be in you which was also in Christ Jesus . . . who emptied himself . . . obedient unto death . . . therefore God raised him and conferred upon him a name above all names" (2:5–10).

As Jeremiah reminded us in his Lamentations (3:25), "The Lord is good to those who wait for him, to the soul that seeks him. It is good that we should wait for the salvation of the Lord."

Since my first experience at the Benediction of the Blessed Sacrament, Merton has helped me to understand that the deepest level of communication is communion and not conversation. Like Merton, I have been in a continuous search for an experience of God, in search for that interior peace which I sense I need in order to be a functioning integrated whole person in community. At first I had difficulty understanding how he could reconcile his monastic life and his commitment to a troubled, sick, impoverished world. I have learned since that deep intimate union with God and self has as a precondition solitude, silence, and a certain separation from the world. And I have learned that it is only from such experiences of unity with God, self, humanity, and the natural world that I am driven and empowered to search for new ways to bind humanity together in love, justice, and peace.

The awareness of consciousness necessary to understand the world's anguish and share in its struggle for healing and fulfillment results from moments spent in what appears to be escape. Surely we need to acknowledge that our engagements in the world do not necessarily bring about true human life or community. Merton boldly emphasized that we cannot live in human community if we do not love one another and that we cannot love one another unless we know and are loved by God, and thereby can love ourselves. Our ability to love our neighbor comes from our communion with God in contemplative prayer.

I am just beginning to understand why *Shabbat* (Sabbath) was so important to our foreparents and why it is the only strictly religious command among the Ten Commandments, and why its fulfillment was insisted upon by the otherwise antiritualistic prophets.

Shabbat is misunderstood if it is seen as only a day of rest, recreation, and freedom from the burdens of work. We have made the Sabbath into a day to sleep late, perhaps go to church, have a big brunch, and engage in family activities or watch the ball games on T.V. Of course Sunday is not *Shabbat*. Sunday is not intended as a day of rest; it is the first day of creation. Still Christians need a *Shabbat*, a day kept holy by doing nothing except being open to God. *Shabbat* is a day of rest insofar as it seeks to reestablish complete harmony between all of creation and God. On this day, nothing must be destroyed or built. *Shabbat* is a day of truce in the human battle with the world. On *Shabbat*, we live as if we possess nothing and everything, we seek only to be. *Shabbat* is a day of joy, because on this day we are fully ourselves. *Shabbat* and the contemplative life go together, just as the Sunday Eucharist feast and the active life go together. Both are dimensions of human existence. Each depends on the other. Regretfully we Christians have tended to distort both.

Christianity has a long contemplative tradition. According to the New Testament, Jesus often withdrew to be alone. The early desert fathers developed a wide range of contemplative techniques. In the Eastern Christian church a practice known as *Hesychasonas*, a means of achieving "divine quietness," emerged. *Hesychasonas* is a process using the name of Jesus as a mantra to accompany our breathing so that we might see the inner light of transfiguration.

It was a long time ago now. I had almost forgotten. Georges Florovski, a Russian Orthodox priest, was my adviser at Harvard Divinity School. One day he confided to a group of us that he did not understand our Western ways of praying. We spent so much time concentrating on the words. The only time you really pray, he explained, is when you are rattling off the words and pay no attention to them for then you can be with God. And is not the aim of prayer to be in God's presence and hear God's voice speak through images and emotions? It seemed strange in those days for my understandings of spirituality were so intellectual and moral.

It was a few years later that I read Salinger's book, *Franny and Zooey*. It is a tale about the life of prayer. At one point it introduces the oldest prayer of the Eastern church, the so-called Jesus prayer, two words *"Kyrie Eleison"* or in English, "Lord Jesus, have mercy on me." As such it is a mantra, a series of words to be repeated over and over again so as to occupy the conscious mind and free the unconscious to experience union with God. Franny says to Zooey,

> If you keep saying that prayer over and over again you only do it with your lips at first then eventually what happens the prayer becomes self-active. Something happens after a while and the words get synchronized with your heartbeat and breathing and then you are actually praying without ceasing.

The purpose, explains Zooey, is Christian consciousness.

In more recent times this ancient prayer mantra of the church has become important for my contemplative life. It continues to be a help as I seek to withdraw and enter the depths of my being. I have used other aids. One is an Eastern Christian retreat known as a *poustinia*. Its purpose is to help us experience the desert, that lonely silent secluded place where God cares for us. When I first went on a *poustinia*, I took with me a pitcher of water, a loaf of bread, a candle, some matches, and a Bible. I went to a small, windowless room with only a mattress on the floor. For forty-eight hours I was alone in that room. I read my Bible by the light of the candle and lying prostrate on the floor waited in the dark silence for God to come. It was in those moments of self-emptying or what might appear to be escape that I found enlightenment and unity with God, myself, and all humanity.

Another help has been learning to pray the Rosary. For those of you unfamiliar with this amazing devotional exercise, it is a combination of a long, complex, but easily remembered mantra, "Hail Mary, full of grace. The Lord is with you. Blessed are you among women and blessed is the fruit of your womb, Jesus. Holy Mary, mother of God, pray for us now and in the hour of our death." It is intended to open our unconscious mind while focusing our conscious minds on a series of meditations: one series is on the joyful mysteries (the Annunciation, the Visitation, the Nativity, Jesus' presentation in the temple, and Jesus being found at the temple); another, the sorrowful mysteries (the agony in the garden, scourging of Jesus, the event of the crown of thorns, carrying his cross on the way to Golgotha, and Jesus' crucifixion); and the third on the glorious mysteries (the Resurrection, Ascension, Coming of Holy Spirit at Pentecost, the Assumption of Mary, and the Glory of the Saints). By enhancing and enlivening our imaginations it helps us be present to God's action in human life and history. There is probably no more perfect prayer in the sense that it brings together in method and content every aspect of our Christian spiritual tradition.

Holding onto a bead to remind myself where I am in my prayer, I repeat the "Hail Mary" mantra ten times, once for each bead. As I repeat this mantra, I focus my imagination on an event in the life of Jesus and become present to it. At the close of this meditation there is a large bead which provides me with a moment to pray the Lord's Prayer and remind myself that the purpose of my prayers is to open myself to God's healing, nurturing presence that I might know and do his will to the end that his kingdom comes. Then I move on to the next meditation. At the end of a cycle of five meditations, I come to the cross on which I reaffirm my baptismal faith through the Apostles' Creed, that is, I once again give my loyalty, my heart, my love to God. Then it is on to the next cycle or series of mysteries until I have completed all three mysteries.

I look forward to the day that I can keep a meaningful weekly *Shabbat*. For the present, I experience them only on retreat or during a few moments in a busy day. I also look forward to the day when I can simply live a contemplative life without the aids I have for the present found helpful. In any case, I have learned that actualization or human life in wholeness is dependent upon a contemplative dimension to balance my active life. I wish I had learned that earlier.

CHAPTER FIVE

Journeying
Beginnings and Endings

JOHN EUSDEN

One of the most important books I have used in my teaching is *Zen Mind, Beginner's Mind* by Shunryu Suzuki. The book has had a continuing influence on me as a teacher; it has stimulated and inspired the minds of my students. Suzuki wrote the book as a series of *teisho*, or brief, informal talks on Zen meditation and practice. It is, in my understanding, the best book on Zen in the English language. And I would like to share my experience as a reader and a teacher.

Shunryu Suzuki came to America in 1958 when he was fifty-three. It was to be a temporary stay, but he was consumed by the genuine American interest in Zen and decided to remain. He said that Americans questioned Zen in a way that gave Zen life. Among the many centers in California that owe their beginning to Suzuki's imagination, energy, and teaching, is Zen Mountain Center at Tassajara Springs above Carmel Valley. Shunryu died of cancer in late 1971. I never met him, although we had correspondence. And I never had a chance to visit Tassajara during his lifetime—my experiences in Zen being rooted in either Japan or on the East Coast. Richard Baker was installed as Suzuki's *dharma*, or teaching, heir shortly before the master's death. At Suzuki's funeral, Baker-*roshi* spoke these words:

There is no easy way to be a teacher or a disciple . . .
no easy way to come to a land without Buddhism and
leave it having brought many disciples, priests, and
laymen well along the path and having changed the
lives of thousands of persons throughout this country
. . . . But this "no-easy-way," this extraordinary accom-
plishment, rested easy with him, for he gave us from
his own true nature, our true nature. He left us as
much as any man can leave, everything essential, the
mind and heart of Buddha.

The overwhelming experience I have each year in teaching *Zen Mind, Beginner's Mind* is the grasping once again
of the meaning of a journey. Suzuki, in masterful, simple
illustration and discourse, focuses not only on the beginning and ending of a journey but, in true Zen style, on the
middle. The book deals with *zazen*, meditation; the ending
of which Suzuki speaks is really the beginning of practice.
To be meditative we must leave the world as we know it,
with its appointments, its busy-ness, its interruptions, its
franticness.

The person practicing *zazen* moves away from judgment
and categories; she searches for her "true mind." The practitioner ends her concern with goals and targets; she does
not live in or for expectations, even of enlightenment; she
pursues the practice because it is good in and of itself at
the moment. In Zen, there is to be no vanity of doing "in
order to."

One begins *zazen* only when one is willing to end other
frenetic ways of life. To be sure, the book does speak of
"going toward something." But that goal is never an identifiable target; it is the sense of being caught up in a process
within which distinctions fade, such as form and content,
good and bad, space and time, even living and dying.
Zazen begins the process toward an understanding of non-
duality. The practice invites us to engage in such a journey.

In living with *Zen Mind, Beginner's Mind* and teaching it

during many semesters, I have been able to appropriate Shunryu Suzuki's overwhelming concern for beginning. A delicate Chinese painting shows a graceful bridge spanning a short stretch of water and a path leading away from the bridge. The painting, with its high arching sky and its sense of spaciousness, presents to the viewer an openness and an invitation. The caption reads, in translation: "A ten-thousand-mile journey begins here." Not only is a new beginning exciting and full of promise—a beginning is the journey itself and even the ending. Beginners start a journey with full attention; they are ready for anything; they offer themselves to the journey as they are. The brusque, beautiful calligraphy of the book's frontispiece, done by Suzuki, reads *shoshin,* or beginner's mind. The Zen way of calligraphy is to write in the most direct natural way, offering what skill you have, not trying to make something exquisite, but rather reflecting your concentration and interest of the moment.

Beginner's mind also depends on innocence. The direct, uncomplicated question at the beginning of meditative practice—what am I?—is the main concern. But it is also the question that is needed throughout the journey of Zen practice. It is the mind that is empty of all things, ready to try all things, willing to live with doubt. It is the mind that can see things as they are and in a flash makes connections and sees the original nature of all things. The advice of the book is "Always be a beginner! Beginner's mind is Zen mind."

But the path that leads across the "ten-thousand-mile bridge" and beyond is not easy. Although we enter into the journey with enthusiasm, concentration, and genuineness, the journey is not guaranteed to be safe or even intelligible. Shunryu Suzuki calls our attention over and over again to the need for practice and even to the need of rules. *Zazen,* meditation, is structured and has its own procedure and unfolding. A practice, a way, procedures, rules are all necessary. They do not mean we are always under control. But, as Suzuki says, "As long as you have rules, you have a chance for freedom. To try to obtain freedom without being aware of the rules means nothing." Just as one must keep on walking on the path across the bridge, one must keep on sitting according to the practice and the way. There will be times of great uneasiness, questioning, inner opposition. Do not expect an easy journey.

Shunryu Suzuki speaks repeatedly about what is going on in the midst of the journey. Beginner's mind can apply to each stage along the way—being ready to encounter newness, greeting each occurrence with enthusiasm and an open mind, living each moment to the fullest. The journey provides us with a chance to enter totally into the meaning of each moment. "Now" is at the heart of things. If we live in each moment fully we see the *dharma*, the reality or teaching, from within; most often we have only a chance to look at reality from the outside. When we live in each moment totally, we also gain a sense of control and direction; we are no longer insignificant lookers-on; we are at the helm, fully conscious of movement and meaning.

Shunryu Suzuki calls to our attention the psychic and spiritual fact that each moment gives way to another on a journey. We do not cling to that which has been but move forward to that which will be present. We do not hold on nostalgically to moments of great meaning in the past. Here Zen makes its parallel to Freudian psychoanalysis—to live in nostalgia is to live in regression. To live holding on to that event, experience, or relationship which once seemed to be so important is not to have beginner's mind! Furthermore, nothing lasts forever. In beginner's mind, we practice nonattachment. The journey is the reality and calls for our participation in it fully at each stage. Consider two Zen *haiku:*

> The long night;
> The sound of the water
> Says what I think.
>
> The stars on the pond;
> Again the winter shower
> Ruffles the water.

The long, still night not only does not last but it is interrupted by the sound of dripping water. The reflection of the stars on the pond is really momentary, for the next shower or puff of wind ruffles the surface.

I have been caught up, recast, and reinvolved time and again by Shunryu Suzuki's *Zen Mind, Beginner's Mind.* Two other books have been influential for me in thinking about journeying and beginnings and endings. John Dunne in *The Way of All the Earth* speaks of insights and understandings gained at points along the journey from one religious tradition to another. My friend and colleague Mark C. Taylor in *Journeys to Selfhood: Hegel and Kierkegaard* considers imaginatively the presence of beginnings in endings and the reverse as he writes about the parallels and differences in the quest of each of these philosophers for the meaning of selfhood.

In all our journeys, we need to keep beginner's mind. At the beginning of any journey, there is no thought of having attained anything. Our mind is open, ready to receive all things compassionately. In all new departures— marriage, a first job, a different spiritual practice or insight, a new work—we should be able to celebrate our boundlessness. This original boundless mind of the beginner can be with us at all other stages along the journey as well. Again, Shunryu Suzuki advises us: Always be a beginner. This is the real secret of not only our spiritual and psychic lives, but also of the arts. We believe, as this book maintains, that most of our spiritual conceptions and proclamations can best be understood in the arts—through dance, painting, representations of our fantasies, music, poetry. We need to practice the unlimitedness of beginner's mind which befits the arts.

The Zen concentration on beginning and on enthusiasm is echoed in our scriptural tradition. The prophets and Jesus speak over and over again about new departures with no indication of the details of the goal or the end. Begin the new journey and the ending will become known to you in the start. Jeremiah records his call in this way: "Now the word of the Lord came to me saying, 'Before I formed you in the womb I knew you, and before you were born I consecrated you; I appointed you a prophet to the nations.' Then I said, 'Our Lord God! Behold I do not know how to speak, for I am only a youth.' But the Lord said to me, 'Do not say, "I am only a youth"; for to all whom I send you you shall go. . .'" (Jer. 1:4–7). Jesus's call to his disciples catches the radical possibility and limitlessness of a beginning. "The next day again John was standing with two of his disciples; and he looked at Jesus as he walked, and said, 'Behold, the Lamb of God!' The two disciples heard him say this, and they followed Jesus. Jesus turned, and saw them following, and said to them, 'What do you seek?' And they said to him, 'Rabbi (which means Teacher), where are you staying?' He said to them, 'Come and see' " (John 1:35–39). Philip's becoming a disciple likewise stresses a terse, boundless beginning. "The next day Jesus decided to go to Galilee and he found Philip and said to him, 'Follow me' " (John 1:43).

Zen Mind, Beginner's Mind speaks to me about the possibility of many journeys—even that of traveling from my own tradition to another and returning. I am attracted to the figure of Buddha and to the figure of Jesus. I am making journeys constantly from the one to the other, recognizing their differences, celebrating the unique forms of religious life which each contributes. Buddha is very cul-

tured, very refined. He is a person who belongs in the
court of a king. Jesus comes from a village, a carpenter's
son—uneducated, uncultured. Buddha is a scholar, steeped
in the wisdom of the Vedic tradition. Jesus, on the other
hand, is like wilderness—raw, vibrant, rebellious. Very
few persons were ever offended by Buddha. Many people,
especially those in authority and those of tradition, were
offended by Jesus. Buddha is a faraway peak; Jesus is the
ground trembling beneath our feet. The wisdom and the
teaching which comes from each are different. Each strain
is a part of me. I journey from one to the other and back
again. It can only be done with beginner's mind—open,
ready, receptive.

Shunryu Suzuki in his remarkable book reminds us,
perhaps most emphatically of all, that on each journey,
whatever its nature, we should catch things as they are at
each point along the route. We pause with a beginner's
mind in order to recognize the fullness of each moment
and event on each journey. In the middle of our most
significant journey, that of life itself, we pause with a
beginner's mind to know that we are in the middle of a
living-dying journey. We live, but we do not always live;
we die, but we do not die. The joining together of life and
death as we think about ourselves on each journey is a way
of catching things truly as they are—of knowing that nonbe-
ing goes hand in hand with being.

Suzuki and the whole Zen tradition remind us of seeing
even the most particular seemingly minute things just as
they are. "Don't think, but look," as the philosopher Witt-
genstein once said to his students. Vincent Persichetti, a
contemporary American composer, has written a "Winter
Cantata for Women's Chorus, Flute and Marimba" in which
the text is taken entirely from Zen *haiku*. Persichetti always requests that this cantata be the last piece on a program. The *haiku* chosen point to the Zen insistence on
immersion in the moment, the taking in fully of a particu-

lar event, and the joy of seeing into something, completely. Here are three:

> A copper pheasant wakes with shrill-edged cry:
> The silver crescent cuts the chilly sky.

> One umbrella, as snowy dusk draws on,
> Has come, and passes by, and now is gone.

> The winter's fitful gusts, as they expire,
> Bring enough fallen leaves to build a fire.

JOHN WESTERHOFF

I will long remember my first confession. It was in the
chapel of the Episcopal cathedral in St. Louis, Missouri.
My confessor was my bishop; the day was the occasion of
my becoming a priest in the Episcopal church. It seemed
like an appropriate time for I was at a new place in my
pilgrimage and beginnings require endings. The Rite of
Reconciliation now has become a regular and essential
part of my life of ever new and growing experiences of
conversions, reconciliation, of healing and restored relationships with God, myself, and my neighbors.

I began by saying: "Pray for me a sinner." My bishop
shared some comforting words of Scripture and bid me
make my confession. I prayed, "Holy God, heavenly Father, you formed me from the dust in your image and
likeness and redeemed me from sin and death by the cross
of your son Jesus Christ. Through the water of baptism
you clothed me with the shining garments of his right-
eousness and established me among your children in your
kingdom. But I have squandered the inheritance of your
saints and have wandered far in a land that is waste. Especially I confess to you and to the church. . . ."

Having made my confession, I was asked if I would
"turn again to Christ as my Lord" and "forgive those who
have sinned against me." Then laying his hands on my
head, my bishop, through the authority committed to him

by God and the church, absolved me from all my sins. Following his words: "The Lord has put away all your sins," I exclaimed, "Thanks be to God." We shared the kiss of peace and he said to me, "Abide in peace and pray for me a sinner."

James Fenhagen, in *More Than Wanderers*, writes:

> A God seeker is a person on a journey. When the thirst has been awakened, we are no longer persons wandering aimlessly about, but persons who have begun to discern the bare outlines of a path. We become more than wanderers. It is a journey based upon the assumption that there is more to life than meets the eye.

Once I witnessed a baptism in a small church in a Latin American village. The community had gathered; they had recalled God's gracious acts; they had proclaimed the good news of God in Jesus Christ. And now they were about to make a response. The congregation began to sing a mournful tune appropriate to a funeral as a solemn procession moved down the aisle. A father carried a child's coffin he had made; a mother carried a bucket of water from the family well; the godparents carried the sleeping infant wrapped only in a native blanket. The father placed the coffin on the altar, the mother poured the water into the coffin, and the priest took the baby from the godparents, covered the baby's skin with embalming oil. The singing softened to a whisper. The priest slowly lowered the infant into the coffin and immersed the child's head in the water. As he did so, he exclaimed, "I kill you in the name of the Father and of the Son and of the Holy Spirit."

"Amen!" shouted the parents and the congregation.

Then quickly lifting the child into the air for all to see, the priest declared, "And I resurrect you that you might love and serve the Lord."

Immediately the congregation broke into a joyous Easter

hymn. But it was not over yet. The priest covered the child with the oils of birth; he dressed the child in a beautiful homemade white robe. Once again the singing quieted as the priest, anointing the child, made the sign of the cross on the child's forehead and said, "I brand you with the sign of Christ so that you and the world will always know who you are and to whom you belong." As the singing continued, the people came forward to share the Kiss of Peace with the newest member of their family.

Baptism is the beginning of a long pilgrimage. Indeed, baptism is a pilgrimage. Herb Brokering, a Lutheran pastor and my friend, once told me about a baptism in which he participated. He was visiting a church in Texas. The people had told him there was to be a baptism while he was with them. "Who's the child?" he asked. "Israel. His parents were born in Mexico," they replied.

Herb had never been to Mexico, but since he was only a few miles from the border he went to buy Israel a gift for his baptism. He saw a pair of sandals he liked, but they were for a ten-year-old. He told the woman about Israel's baptism and she said, "Don't worry, he'll grow into them."

Israel slept during the baptism. He didn't see Herb give him the sandals or tell the story, but his father and mother were wide awake and understood.

Two months later Herb returned to this church. He discovered that Lisa, Israel's cousin, was to be baptized. He went looking for another pair of sandals. He fell in love with a pair of booties, but they were much too small. He told the woman about Lisa's baptism and the woman said, "Don't worry. Tell her to hang them on the wall to remind her she was baptized." And that's what he did.

Baptism is living between remembering and growing into. Baptism is both having arrived and going somewhere; it is getting a new start and going on a pilgrimage.

In the Christian liturgy baptism is the sacrament of beginnings, of what Christians call justification. Justification is God's act of setting right, of providing new life for those who have lost its meaning and purpose. Justification is God's reestablishment of the possibility of human life in its fullness, it is God restoring human life to its original intent. But justification is just the beginning for the Christian. The journey or pilgrimage which follows is known as sanctification. Sanctification implies continuing change and growth, a journey of beginnings and endings. Sometimes it is slow and gradual, sometimes rapid and spontaneous, sometimes serendipitous, and sometimes cultivated. It is a process of maturation, of actualization or becoming who in point of fact we already are. To be sanctified is to be in the process of becoming the person we are and were created to be. Each and every actualization opens up a new possibility for further actualization.

On one occasion Thomas Merton was asked by a Buddhist monk, "What do your vows oblige you to do?" Merton is said to have replied, "I believe they can be interpreted as a commitment to a total inner transformation of one sort or another, a commitment to become a completely new person." The aim of our pilgrimage is to be transformed from within that we might perceive reality in a new way, experience the world in a new way and live our lives in relationship to that world in ways that God's will might be done and God's kingdom comes. For that to occur our journey has endings and beginnings.

Conversions, the change of mind or perception, the repentance to which a Christian is called, is a continuous and lifelong process. While conversions begin as everything in history does at some time, their processes are not completed until every aspect of the human personality is driven out into the light of God's mercy and renewed. Conversions proceed layer by layer, relationship by relationship, here a little, there a little—until the whole personality, intellect, feeling, and will have been recreated by God.

Conversion refers not only to the initial moment of faith, no matter how dramatic or revolutionary it may seem, but to the whole life of the believer and the network of relationships in which that life is entangled: personal, familial, social, economic, and political. That is why the church is called a school. Faith is not something we have, it is something we learn. Conversion is not only the little wicket gate through which Bunyan's pilgrim quickly passes as he abandons the City of Destruction; it is the entire pilgrimage of the Celestial City.

No aspect of thinking on conversion is more foreign to the American evangelical experience than this stress on conversion as a process rather than a crisis. Evangelicals emphasize emotion and an initial movement. This moment is celebrated, recalled, and when the experience fades, recaptured. But Christian tradition does not agree.

Baptism is more like a cowl or such a garment that is given to a novice. The young boy of twelve is a Franciscan from the very moment he accepts the cowl and the obligations wearing it entails. But he is not a Franciscan in the same sense as an old brother of eighty-two who has worn the brown robe of St. Francis all his long and varied life. The young novice must grow into the cowl he has been given. So too with baptism. We must grow into it. We do so as we are continually converted at even deeper levels of our personality.

That explains why in the Episcopal Church's *Book of Common Prayer* (1979), baptism is to be celebrated five times each year: at the Easter Vigil, on the Day of Pentecost, All Saints' Day, the Feast of the Baptism of our Lord, and the Visitation of the Bishop. Whether or not there are any candidates for baptism the community renews its baptismal vows. Over and over again throughout our journey, we need to renounce the power of evil and recommit ourselves to Jesus Christ, we need to reaffirm our faith and our promises to continue in the apostles' teaching and fellowship, in the breaking of bread, and in the prayers; to persevere in resisting evil, and whenever we fall into sin repent and return to the Lord; to proclaim by word and example the Good News of God in Christ; to seek and serve Christ in all persons, loving our neighbor as ourselves; and to strive for justice and peace among all people, respecting the dignity of every human being.

The devotional exercise that most vividly encourages and fosters in me an active sharing in the life and ministry of our Lord is known as the Stations or Way of the Cross. In this devotion through our imaginations we walk with Jesus along the way to Calvary, we take up our cross and follow him. In the earliest days the Christian faith was known as "the way"; it is a way of life. Faith is not simply a matter of the intellect. It involves the totality of our life, our intellects, our emotions, our wills. Insofar as Christian life is the way of a pilgrim, it is summed up in the Way of the Cross, and this devotion helps us to shape lives accordingly.

To go on the Way of the Cross is to experience a new beginning. This devotion has played an important role in my journey. For those of you who may never have used this devotion, it is comprised of fourteen stations: Jesus is condemned to death, Jesus takes up his cross, Jesus falls the first time, Jesus meets his afflicted mother, the cross is laid on Simon of Cyrene, a woman wipes the face of Jesus, Jesus falls a second time, Jesus meets the women of Jerusalem, Jesus falls a third time, Jesus is stripped of his garments, Jesus is nailed to the cross, Jesus dies on the cross, the body of Jesus is placed in the arms of his mother, and Jesus is laid in the tomb.

At each Station, we say alone or with others, "We adore you, O Christ, and we bless you; Because by your holy cross you have redeemed the world." Then in our imagination we go to that place on the Way and relive it. We sense where that hurt is in our life and let Christ share it with us; we sense where others are sharing that hurt and we discern how we might bring healing to them. Each meditation is followed by a prayer of thanksgiving and commitment and then we go to the next Station, singing "Holy God, Holy and Mighty, Holy Immortal One, Have mercy on us." We participate in the Way of the Cross through formal readings, meditations and prayers, or informally following the same intentions. In either case, it is an experience of refreshment and renewal on our way toward sanctification.

John MacQuarrie, in his book *Paths in Spirituality*, distinguishes three levels upon which we enter the Christian pilgrimage. These three levels correspond to the three stages by which classical spirituality described the Christian way. The Purgative Way—discovering and acknowledging who we really are and what we are to become; The Illuminative Way—our growth in understanding this commitment and its implications; and The Unitive Way—union with God in Christ or the actualization of life.

During this first stage of our journey, as we stand before the First Station, for example, which depicts Jesus being condemned to death, we can identify with those who do not understand and make our first step toward accepting the mystery of grace and salvation. To respond to this grace is to become disciples. Then, in the second stage, at the Fifth Station, for example, we meet Simon of Cyrene who takes Christ's cross from him and at the Sixth, St. Veronica, who administers to Jesus' suffering. Now we can identify with them and discern how we are being called to live in the world. Then at the final stage of union with Christ, we come, for example, to the Thirteenth Station, where the body of Jesus is placed in the arms of his mother. Here we can identify with her and realize that we, too, are pregnant with God and so can become aware of what it means to live so that others, by looking at us, will catch a glimpse of their own potential.

Another devotional exercise I have found helpful is a way of praying the Lord's Prayer. It was taught to me by Sister Chris Gelling, a colleague who directs Avila, a retreat center in Durham, North Carolina. For the Christian, prayer is essentially listening and responding to God. God wishes to tell us what to pray for. If we pray accordingly we can be assured that God has already answered our prayer. Essential to our journey of beginnings and endings is this life of prayer. If we see each petition in the Lord's Prayer as instructing us in what questions to ask so that when we pray in the spirit of the prayer, we request from God that which God intends for us, we can grow in grace.

To pray the Lord's Prayer in this way is to take each petition, bring its question before God, listen until we have a sense of what God wants us to request; then to request what God has revealed to us and pass on to the next petition in confidence that our prayer has already been answered. To pray the Lord's Prayer in this manner is to bring these questions before God: Our Father in Heaven (what do you want to make possible for me this day that neither I nor any other human being can make possible?); Hallowed be your name (what do you want to make holy in my life this day?); Your kingdom come (how can your kingdom come through me this day?); Your will be done on earth as in heaven (what are my Gethsemanes about which I need to say your will be done); Give us this day our daily bread (what nourishment or help do I need most this day?); Forgive us our sins as we forgive those who sin against us (for what do I need most to be forgiven and who do I need most to forgive?); Save us from the time of trial and deliver us from evil (from what do I need most to be protected this day?).

Some of my most meaningful and transformed experiences of prayer have come from engaging in this devotion.

The spiritual life is a pilgrimage or journey. Luther reminded us that we are to live into our baptism. It is a pilgrimage of new beginnings and growing up, of conversions and nurture. It is difficult to remember that. It is even more difficult to do it. Living a penitential life of participation in the church's rites of reconciliation has become an essential part of my journey of beginnings and endings. Through my regular confessions to a priest who in the midst of the confessional not only makes real God's reconciliation by announcing the grace of absolution but offers me guidance, counsel, and spiritual direction, I am able to grow in my spiritual life.

One other daily spiritual exercise has helped me. The examination of consciousness is a fivefold meditation exercise intended to help pilgrims on their journey. It begins by remembering and reliving in your imagination a moment in your life when you experienced grace. It then turns to a review of the last twenty-four hours and a search for those moments when you have experienced brokenness and incompleteness in your life, to those experiences through which God is calling you to wholeness and health. Aware of those gaps in your life, it asks you to bring them before God's transforming presence; to ask God to heal you. It then requires that you listen, to discover the new health and wholeness toward which God is calling you and to give yourself to that awareness as you make a commitment to its implied way of life. And last it closes with a thankful celebration of this new grace in your life.

As Rachel Hosmer and Alan Jones point out in *Living in the Spirit* the images and metaphors most helpful to the Christian journey are being chosen, making new beginnings, and growing up. Christians have always believed that they have no advantages in this world or the next. They have been mysteriously chosen by God to so live that others might know what is true for them also. Christians are simply those who have been given the gift of faith or sight to perceive the truth about humanity and human life. They are thereby called to be *for* the not-yet-chosen; to be a sign that God chooses us all. In the end God chooses all peoples through the one chosen people.

To actualize our human condition and fulfill our calling to wholeness and holiness of life calls for a life of continual transformations or new beginnings and of growing up. Conversion invokes changes in the way we look at the world, at others, at ourselves, and at the things we think matter. To turn and to live in response to the call of God is to be human. It is a continuing process. So is our growth in maturity of faith and life. We need to grow into our new perceptions. We need to actualize our true human condition as a chosen, redeemed people. It is a slow and gradual pilgrimage of beginnings and endings.

CHAPTER SIX

Everydayness
Life Alone and Together

JOHN EUSDEN

It was a cold January afternoon. Ice was underfoot and the wind was whistling in the trees—and going right through our jackets. We were carrying all our gear up to a remote cabin in a large private forest in western Vermont—sometimes known as the "backside" of the Green Mountains. My students, two other teachers, and I were about to begin a Zen *sesshin*. The word means a retreat, a seclusion, a time of concentration; but it also means in the Japanese an occasion "to touch the mind." The purpose of a *sesshin* is more than turning off the world; a *sesshin* should allow you a chance to confront your "true mind," to search for your true self.

There were twenty-two of us, men and women. We were to live together in the strict discipline of Rinzai Zen, one of the main Japanese divisions of Zen Buddhism. There would be *zazen,* meditation, at dawn, noon, dusk, and midnight. We would practice *aikido* together, concentrating on the loosening exercises and the small movements of this martial art. We would do Taoist walking in a group, conversing about all manner of things on the first half, but maintaining silence on the way back—aware of crunching ice and snow, wind, our bodies, and a different sense of being together. Our meals would be in common, consisting of austere but ample *sesshin* fare—rice, green tea, vegetables, lentil soup, fruit, bread. Each person had one pair of chopsticks, a cup, and a bowl; enough tea was saved in the last serving to rinse and wash all utensils at the table; upon rising, our simple eating equipment was stored in shelves across the room under our names. There was time in our schedule for reading and conversation and some sleeping!

As I entered into the discipline of the *sesshin* I was caught up in the extraordinariness of the ordinary. We were all involved in splitting wood, stove-tending, meal-preparation, and clean-up. These necessary tasks were performed with humor, thoroughness, and elation. We all seemed immersed in the daily living of our common life. Sustaining ourselves so that we could maintain our practice took on special meaning. There is a Zen saying, "Wonder of wonders—I haul firewood; I carry water."

I thought of the Zen spirit present in our common meals. Zen does encompass the totality of life and eating is a part of that totality. Too often we pay little attention to eating and to the preparation of food. When we were servers and preparers, we all found ourselves concerned with the flavor of the food itself and with the entire atmosphere. The utensils on the table, cleanliness, the feeling of the room, the spirit of the servers—all of these are important in the process of eating and exert an influence on the taste of food. When one serves, one does not only place the food before others; one serves one's whole being. To eat does not mean only to fill one's stomach, but to take in with feeling everything that is present—the silence or the conversation, the spirit of the server and the cook, the appearance of the table and its utensils, the warmth of the room, the ice on the windows.

As we became immersed in our ordinary pursuits, we felt a sense of wonder operating. We did not depend only on our bodies and minds for sustenance and inspiration; we allowed the energy of wood, fire, rice, tea, steamed vegetables, spring water to enter our being and become part of us.

The everydayness of the *sesshin* related to more than our feelings about food, water, warmth, and space. During the course of the discipline of the long weekend, all of us rethought the common, ongoing experience of being alone and being together. Even though many of our pursuits were done alone in connection with our quest for "true mind"—meditation, splitting wood, the second half of Taoist walking, reading—we were always immersed in our life in the *sangha,* or community. Each one of us commented upon the fact that energy was shared and concentration given by others when we did *zazen* together. The sense of helping, sharing, participating in a larger rhythm is present when one does meditation with others seated in a circle, either facing empty space in the middle or the blank walls around the room. Meditation by oneself does not have this sense. We were aware of the present always being fresh when humor and guffaws broke out among us. It spontaneously happened that there were no private, in-group jokes; rather our humor appeared always to be invitational and inclusive. In both our shared energy and in our humor we were conscious of the fact that we were more than the sum of our parts, that something accumulative was taking place, and that something we had not expected was happening before our eyes. I was reminded of Buson's *haiku:*

> Lighting one candle
> With another candle
> An evening of spring.

We seemed also to be able to treat each other with respect and understanding for the particular qualities which each possessed. Within the context of our weekend *sangha,* each person seemed to be moving to what he or she could be. I though of the German philosopher Max Scheler who once stated that "Love is that movement wherein each individual object which possesses value achieves the highest value compatible with its nature."

In our times of conversation while drinking tea after *zazen* or after a meal, we spoke of our involvement in the outside world. Those directly participating in the peace movement described their hopes and their fears about nuclear weapons and about outdated diplomacy and international relations. We listened attentively to those who worked in community projects and who were dealing directly with problems of racism and drug addiction.

The *sesshin* experience also taught us to trust our own life energy. Each one of us lived an individual experience as well as a group experience during the retreat. I became very conscious of the Zen insistence that more of myself would be available to others if I examined and dealt with myself more deeply. It became clear to me that I could trust others when I grasped the sense of trusting my own specialness. We were all using the time to work on self-understanding as we searched for that Zen "true mind" of concentration, uniqueness, compassion, and emptiness. In the discipline of the *sesshin*, we discovered the difference between being alone and being lonely. Time used in being alone prepared you to enter more fully into being together. Time which is lonely frightens you and ultimately separates you from others.

I thought about the words of my Indian teacher Rajneesh, who once spoke to us about the intimate *sangha* of man-woman relationships:

> The capacity to be alone is the capacity to love. It may look paradoxical to you but it is not. It is an existential truth: only those people who are capable of being alone are capable of love, of sharing, of going into the deepest core of the other person—without possessing the other, without becoming dependent on the other, without reducing the other to a thing, and without becoming addicted to the other.

The experience of being alone in the *sesshin* reinforced for me the Zen insistence that there are no right, proper, true answers to questions about ourselves when such answers are given by and readily received from others. I think especially of the questioning we should have about "strong advice" and intimidating suggestions offered by parents and teachers. We can be helped, but we must respond to our own needs and our own understanding of the context within which we act. We struggle for this self-knowledge. But when we find it we should proclaim it and live by it.

Basho, the Zen *haiku* poet, wrote:

> I am one
> Who eats his breakfast
> Gazing at the morning-glory.

Our expression and appreciation of beauty should come from deep inside ourselves. We may be aided and encouraged by an art professor, but, in the end, our response to form, lines, emptiness, color is our own.

A young Zen adept was sweeping a rock-and-stone garden leading to a tearoom. Overhead was an enormous maple tree with branches very close to the ground from which leaves were continually dropping. His master came out to inspect the garden and saw it swept absolutely clean. He said, "Oh no, that's too much." He grabbed an overhanging maple branch and sprinkled a few leaves on the ground; he shuffled them around to give a spontaneous and unplanned look.

Just then the father of the young adept who was a famous master in the area cried to his son from just beyond a low stone wall, "Son, lift me over the stone wall so that I may come in to tea." The young man lifted his father over the wall; the father saw the garden and shook his head. He went to the maple branch and shook vigorously, again and again. Finally there were so many leaves in the garden that they were halfway to the ankle.

The adept grew up and became a Zen master himself and a very famous one. And his son studied Zen. Much later the son was sweeping the garden and heard his father call to him over the same wall, "Lift me over the wall so that I may come to tea." The garden had a few leaves sprinkled in it and again looked spontaneous and unplanned. The former adept and now master took a broom and swept it clean.

Which was the right form for the rock-and-stone Zen garden? The answer: Each one who tended the garden must do it in his own way. The important thing is to express what you feel in your mind and your heart about this form of beauty at the time. The garden story reminds us of the psychic and spiritual necessity of finding our own tao, or way. The Zen story also reminds us that each form of the garden has its value. Although we may choose one style when tending the garden, we are called to admire them all.

The Zen *sesshin* in the deep of a Vermont winter had many implications for my own Christian way. We need to pay more attention to the extraordinariness of the ordinary. When we pay attention to and respectfully use simple everyday things, we are connected with God's creating love in our ordinary world. The extraordinary power of such things emerges when we think of their symbolism and their ability to create new thoughts within us. I think of Jeremiah's references to grape vines, a boiling pot, and clay. And Jesus speaks to us of the fig tree and of rocks and stones.

In the majority of the Protestant traditions, developing from Reformation theology, we are continually presented with the meaning of human life together. The ethical theme of responsiveness rightly builds on the premise of our intermingling and connection with others. But too often in Protestant Christianity we talk of losing ourselves—in some great cause, in the second great commandment of

"Love your neighbor as yourself," in service to the church. We think that in losing ourselves we will find ourselves— no matter how mixed up, how undisciplined, how insensitive our "selves" are. We do not speak of the value of the quest that comes from being alone—of knowing ourselves before God, of finding our Christian "true mind." There are many meanings to Jesus' parable about the mote or speck that is in one's neighbor's eye and the beam or log that is in one's own eye. One meaning is that we will always live in an escapist, even harmful, do-goodism if we do not search for our own integrity, needs, possibilities, and hopes. Let's take the beam or the log out of our own eye and discover, at least in a beginning sense, who we are and what we can be and do, before we lose ourselves in the service of others. Let's see into ourselves and then catch the vision of loving our neighbor.

When God called Abram to be a patriarch and a leader in Genesis 12, Abram was commanded to go from his own country and kindred and father's house to a land that would be shown to him. The Hebrew in the beginning of the charge in verse 1 reads, "Go forth to yourself." Only when Abram came to know himself before God, recognizing his inadequacies and yet his powers, was he able to lead his people and leave his country, his kindred, and his father's house for a new land.

JOHN WESTERHOFF

In class one day, I invited everyone to be silent, to relax and be open to the Spirit. Don't try to do or achieve anything, I advised, just for fifteen minutes. One student came up to me after class to complain that he was not paying tuition to sit in class and do nothing. The next day, after I had described the weekend retreat that was a course requirement, another student made an appointment to see me. He explained that he was a student pastor and therefore could not go on the retreat. I asked why and he told me he was expected to be at church. Thinking the problem was authority, I told him I would write him an excuse. Then he said, "You don't understand. I have a lot of things I must do. I don't have time to go off and do nothing." I tried my best to help him understand that his parishioners needed him to tell them he was going to pray and that if he didn't take time for retreat he would eventually have nothing to bring to them. He dropped the course.

Still some of my students tell me that the silence we have at the opening of class is among the most meaningful learning times in their daily routine. Others have confided that the retreats provide them with their most significant educational experiences and make all their active lives acquire meaning and purpose. My own experience substantiates these truths.

A number of years ago I spent two weeks living in a monastery. It was an experience of moving into a different world. There were many differences, of course, but the most fundamental was that we lived from sunrise to sunset governed by a life of prayer, in solitude and in community.

A structured day was not a new experience. My days were always ordered. I woke up without an alarm at 6:00 A.M. every day. I continually wore a watch and lived by the clock. My daily calendar was marked off in fifteen-minute segments. I knew what a daily round ordered by responsibilities and work was all about, but I had never experienced life ordered by prayer. It was the most liberating experience of my life.

Most of the days I spent alone: each day I worked in the monastery garden, took a hike and a swim in a pool formed by a mountain stream; studied in the monastery library; and meditated. The only times the community gathered were when bells called us to corporate prayers at regular three-hour intervals from six in the morning through nine in the evening and for meals, which were eaten in prayerful silence. In this environment, I experienced a new sense of life lived in the presence of God where there was meaningful solitude and community and centeredness of life. I could not stay at the monastery, for God had made clear to me that this was not where I was to live out my journey in faith. But there I learned what everydayness could be like whether alone or with others when it is lived in prayer.

Within Judaism the basic unit of time is the seven-day week for which Genesis I indicated the liturgical significance in each day. Days were marked by a morning and evening sacrifice and corporate worship consisting of Psalms and prayers at nine in the morning and three in the afternoon. Devout Jews also marked three times of the day with private prayers, before bed, at rising, and at noon.

The early Christians organized each week around Sunday. Each day, following Genesis I, maintained a special significance, but each day took on a new meaning. Sunday was the day of creation; it was also the day of resurrection or new creation. Monday emphasized the unity of all life with God in Jesus Christ. Tuesday stressed dependence on God for life. Wednesday celebrated the conviction that all time and history belonged to God and that it was within history that Christ acts to bring into reality God's kingdom. Thursday focused upon our human unity with all creation and that the action of God in Jesus Christ was for all humanity. Friday reminded them of our human genesis and of the fact that we were all born to die. Saturday was a day of resting in the Lord and of patient, trustful waiting for the resurrection.

The early church retained the practice of marking each day with morning and evening corporate prayer. The morning service was a liturgy of the Word consisting of readings, instruction, and prayer. All who were able were expected to be present for this daily liturgy. Those who could not be present were expected to study the Scriptures and pray at this same hour wherever they were. The evening service, which included psalmody, prayer, and readings, was introduced by a blessing of the lights and sometimes was followed by a simple meal of *agape*.

At the beginning of the day, Luther maintained, it is important to remember that God will be with us all day directing our lives and sustaining us in our labor. At the close of the day he reminded us that we need to reflect on our faithfulness during the day just passed and to ask God to protect us through the night and bring us to a new faithfulness in the new day. Lutherans, Anglicans, and Roman Catholics have, to greater and lesser degree, maintained the importance of daily common prayer for Christian life, that is, of taking time each day to sing praises and thanksgivings to God, to listen to and reflect on God's Word to us, and to center our attention on God and recognize his presence in our lives. Equally important, these traditions have maintained that we are corporate selves and need to pray with others; that we need to be supported and encouraged in our prayers by the presence of others; and that we need the community to pray with us if our life of prayer is to be vital and not wither through neglect.

In the secular world we are subject to the clock, but our sense of time lacks depth and is often without meaning. Our days are often dull and routine, our labor anesthetizing or harried. We often try to escape time through superficial partying or other activities aimed at dulling our sense of time. There is only the relentless existence of work time and Saturday night fever, a landscape where God is forgotten or only a memory. Our vacations (we do not commonly refer to them as holy days—holidays) do not provide an anticipation of what time might be; instead they only provide us with an escape from time.

The question remains, is it possible for the doctor, the teacher, the parent, the student, the parish priest, the factory worker, the business person—and the rest of us—to know in the disordered world of human affairs anything of that serenity and centeredness that we glimpse during a few precious hours spent on retreat? With duties to perform, trains to catch, and deadlines to meet, how can there be anything like a prayerful ordering of time? Is there any way to experience time in an alternative way to the sense of time by which we usually live? These questions are of course rhetorical. Those whose time is lived daily between the hours of morning and evening prayer, whose lives are marked by moments for personal meditation, can indeed experience an alternative.

When our lives are caught up in time ordered by prayer, personal and corporate, we experience a reality quite different from the pressures and routines of our everyday experience. When we live by a prayerful ordering of time, we feel at home in the universe, and we experience a liberating serenity even in the midst of turmoil and trial.

Persons living under the strains and stresses of the everyday world need, we contend, to find a rule of prayer that will be flexible enough to allow us to meet the incessant and unpredictable demands made upon our time and yet regular enough to provide that spiritual order necessary for sanity and meaning.

The problem with modern secular life with its stresses and strains is that it is lived in isolation from God, from self, from neighbor, and nature. Time threatens to become our enemy. We have no time for it has us. We are eternally busy but the joy of labor eludes us; we are constantly in the presence of other people, but we suffer from loneliness. It was Dietrich Bonhoeffer who warned us, "Let him who cannot be alone beware of community and let him who is not in community beware of being alone." He also reminded us that life alone and in community begins and ends in prayer.

Community is not a human achievement but a divine

gift; it results from the life of solitude and prayer. Henri Nouwen explained how in solitude we grow together. In meditation and prayer we discover each other in ways that physical presence does not make possible. Without solitude we cling to each other. With solitude we learn to depend on God and life together takes on a new character.

For some solitariness points simply and solely to aloneness; absence of involvement in community. But solitude means more than aloneness. As Alfred North Whitehead wrote in *Religion in the Making*, "Religion is what a man does with his solitariness." Solitarism can lead a person to aloneness, despair, and melancholia, and thus many live with an almost demonic passion to avoid solitude and to merge with a crowd. But as Whitehead also said, "If you are never solitary, you are never religious." Genuine solitude can also nurture honesty about ourselves, lead us through prayer into the deepest interior discovery that we are infinitely loved by God, and can bring us into an experience of true community with all humanity. That is why Jesus counseled us to withdraw into a closet to pray.

Recently, while on retreat, I entered a large room set aside for meditation. Its walls were empty except for a single scroll on which was written a verse from Hosea, "I will entice you into the desert and there I will speak to you in the depths of your heart." Since then I have learned that until I have been brought in solitude to the ground of my being, where I am beyond the grip of my surface self with all its distractions, I am not able to hear the divine whisper.

Meditation is withdrawing from the world with its outer and inner barrage of distractions and an opening of the way for prayer that produces profound relationships of depth with myself, with God, and with all other souls.

Solitude produces an emptying—a slipping from the grips of the world's fierce clutch—and a filling, a restoring, of interior space that is wholeness and holiness.

Douglas Steere, the Quaker, tells of writing to Jane Richardson, a nun who lives quietly as a hermit, and asking her how to describe the fruits of solitariness. She responded that solitude taught her that we all share the Great Life of God and that we can touch the lives of others in the Being of God where we are all interrelated. Its fruits have been a sense of rightness about her life, increasing hope of life for everyone, joy and community with sisters and brothers in all places and times.

Solitude and community, like contemplation and action, are interrelated and complementary; they are necessary modes in the rhythm of life. At the heart of both is life informed by prayer.

Of course there is no one way to pray. As Urban Holmes points out in his book *The History of Christian Spirituality*, some have found their life of prayer is more profound when it is speculative, emphasizing the illumination of the mind; others have done so when it is affective, emphasizing the illumination of the heart. Some have found that techniques of meditation that are apophatic, or emptying, are most helpful, and others that techniques that are kataphatic, or imagining, are most helpful. Throughout history there have been many schools of spirituality, each appealing to different people and providing styles of prayer and possibilities for creative dialogue within the person and within the community as it seeks to understand the experience of God and its meaning for everyday life in the world. Wholeness and holiness of life is lived in four modes: intellectual, affective, intuitive, and volitional. A healthy spirituality, of course, maintains a tension among the various emphases, for when it does not we tend to fall into some heresy of excess. That is what the heresies of rationalism or an excessive concern for right thinking, of pietism or an excessive concern for right feeling, of quietism or an excessive concern for escapist otherworldiness, or of moralism or an excessive concern for this worldliness activism are all about. Still we must each find our own way.

For too long we have thought of the Christian life as essentially either involvement in political, economic, social concerns that wear us out and result in depression or activity which keeps the church intact and doctrinally pure. Our primary orientation cannot be to an institution or some great cause or even other people, but first and forever to God. Unless our identity is hid in God we will never know who we are or what we are to do. Our first act must be prayer, *Oratio*. To be human is to pray, to meditate both day and night on the love and activity of God. We are called to be continuously formed and transformed by the thought of God within us. Prayer is a disciplined dedication to paying attention. Without the singleminded attentiveness of prayer we will rarely hear anything worth repeating or catch a vision worth asking anyone else to gaze upon.

Too many of us are thinking these days as the world thinks because we do not begin our thinking by thinking about God. Only by paying attention to God will we experience the ecstasy that leads to wisdom. Prayer is that work, that disciplined attentiveness, that bold losing of oneself, that openness to divine leading which defines the everyday spiritual life of every human being. We are called to work and pray. But if we don't pray, if we don't pay close attention to God, our work becomes drudgery rather than vocation, meaningless rounds of activities rather than meaningful human life, even our actions on behalf of social justice become self-righteous and self-serving rather than a radical witness to true human life.

Prayer is at the heart of the Christian life. Prayer is communion with God, a personal response to God's presence. The Scriptures, meditation, and contemplation are devotional aids to prayer. They aid us in becoming aware of God's presence in history and our lives, in opening ourselves to receive God's ever-present Word, and in responding totally with love toward God and neighbor.

God speaks to us first! This fundamental truth makes it possible for us to pray. God had been concerned for each of us long before we became concerned for ourselves. God desires communication with us! God speaks to us continually in various modes: through Jesus Christ; through the Church and other people; through creation; through the events of our lives; and through the Holy Scriptures.

God invites us to listen! Our response to God's initial move is to enter into a relationship with God that is analogous to human friendships. The following characteristics of friendships need to be practiced regularly, choosing a personally appropriate time of day, place, length of time, and rhythm: time alone; sharing below level of ideas; creative waste; expressions of intimacy; expect nothing in particular; open to others; and listen carefully. The process goes something like this: establish a time and place for silence; relax your body and clear your mind; perform a "reverent" act; enter the presence of God; listen to God; express gratitude for time together; perform a "reverent" act; reflect on your experience and record it in your journal.

Prayer also involves the active use of our imaginations. The powers of the spiritual realm seldom deal with people just on a conscious, rational level. The key that unlocks the door to the inner world is imagination. Images give us a way of thinking that brings us closer to actual experiences of the spiritual world than any concept or merely verbal idea. Images come from the inner world where we have the most intimate contact with realities that are usually hidden from view in the outer world. Various imaginative exercises have helped me.

Biblical Images: I begin by entering a Biblical story in my imagination. By stepping into an actual event or taking part in one of the stories told by Jesus, we can participate in images that are already formed and share in their deepest meaning.

Spontaneous Images: I often wait for images to arise spontaneously from within and then follow them as they move. If they become too threatening or destructive, we can call upon the Risen Christ to support and protect. After all, getting into a real pickle is often the only thing that brings us human beings to find the Christ.

Mood Images: Instead of trying futilely to ignore a bad mood, or going right out to celebrate a good one, I try to enter the mood and allow it to be expressed in images which can then be worked with, again turning to Christ to bring renewed vitality and a sense of direction.

Dream Images: Still another method is to listen to one's dreams, which are a natural expression of the inner world. They come without asking leave or knocking, and seem to vanish again into nowhere. But if their images are given quiet, meditative attention, they can be invited back and figures can even be persuaded to speak of meanings from various levels of our being.

Prayer is honest conversation. The Psalms are a school of prayer that teach us ways of expressing ourselves before God; read aloud a verse or phrase; immediately express aloud whatever feelings or thoughts the Psalm evokes; listen to your own words and God's response; continue in this manner until the Psalm is completed. Further, prayer is encountering God through the Scriptures. The following process can be helpful: read the lessons for the day, read a commentary on the lessons; read the lessons again; enter into the presence of God; simply listen; relive the lesson by entering into it yourself and listen to this encounter with God; become each of the characters in the lesson and let God speak to you through your participation in the lessons; express gratitude for your time with God; reflect and write your reflections in your journal.

More important, however, is this: I discovered the importance of a rhythm in life, a movement from doing to being, between collective work and festivity, from engagement in history to contemplation of eternity, from structured experience and reflective actions to antistructured experience and intuitional symbolic actions, between retreat and political, economic, social life, from solitude and contemplation to activism. Without that rhythm life loses its character and the community we seek with God, self, neighbor and the natural world eludes us.

CHAPTER SEVEN

Salvation
Ends for Life

JOHN EUSDEN

I begin with another experience at the Bhagwan Sri Rajneesh *ashram* in India—that special place which has
produced both puzzlement and illumination for me. I spent
a long weekend retreat at the *ashram* trying to respond to
the words "Tell me who you are." Our group was divided
into pairs, numbering about forty people in all. The de-
mand statement was put to me by a partner. I would enter
a period of concentration on this exercise in self-inquiry
and disclosure and reply to my partner, sitting directly
opposite me. My partner was instructed not to make any
verbal response to my words, but to listen attentively and
maintain "sympathetic eye contact." Roles would reverse,
and I would then direct the same statement to my colleague of the moment.

Hours went by, in the night and in the day; partners
changed; walking in the garden occasionally provided a
respite. We ate sparsely and slept little. But, no matter
what was going on, for two and a half days we were urged
to "stay with our question." Stay with it I did—becoming
bored with it, sometimes laughing at it, hating it, and
occasionally rejoicing in it. A similar exercise is used by
the human potential movement in America, but at Poona,
because of setting and leadership, the practice took on
both a Zen intensity and a Taoist sense of cutting away.

During the concentrated time of examination and decla-
ration, I began to realize that the person I was trying to tell
about was not just the one who grew up with his parents
and two brothers in greater Boston, did graduate work in
religion and philosophy, married and had four children,
spent time in the White Mountains of New Hampshire,
teaches, writes books, appreciates Japanese culture, and
enjoys sports and the sense of being in his body. Indeed,
only when I forgot these things, which seemingly were so
crucial for me, was I able to respond in a deeper way to
"Tell me who you are." It became clear that I was not the
person who had done certain things, but I was the person
to whom things had been presented—many, many things.
The real "I" was the person who looked out and beyond,
who had received much and knew that he would receive
more. The self I was telling about was out there, connected
with and determined by forces and events not of my own
creation.

At the end of the retreat, a Zen saying became imprinted
on my mind, "To forget about the self is to be enlightened
by all things." These words are about salvation. Eastern
religions always speak of egolessness. This primary concern means a moving through and beyond our posses-
sions, desires, achievements, and even judgments—a
discarding of our attachments. It also means having a concern for others, living in the spirit of compassion. The
meaning of being egoless is, most importantly, a movement into the infinite universe that stands before our eyes—
"to be enlightened by all things," as the Zen saying
has it.

Shunryu Suzuki, author of *Zen Mind, Beginner's Mind*
and founder of Tassajara Zen Center in California, writes,
"When we become truly ourselves, we just become a swing-
ing door, and we are purely independent of, and at the
same time, dependent upon everything. . . . Each one of us
is in the midst of myriads of world. We are in the center

of the world always, moment after moment." Salvation is concerned with going out the door into a new and unpredictable world. We are to find our salvation in a surrounding wholeness that is beyond ourselves. The movement of salvation is out and up. Salvation is not reaching down to cling to our status, our wants, and our cravings—not even to our commandments about sisterhood and brotherhood. Basho catches the movement in his haiku:

> Having tumbled off
> His grass-blade
> The firefly
> Buzzes up again.

Salvation means to trust the motion and power of this infinite universe before our eyes. We behold and learn from the world of nature, relationships, and developments and events not caused by ourselves. Part of our ego centeredness is to ascribe motion and cause only to ourselves. But the motion outside is what we should welcome as a true force and teacher. Motion is the essence of reality, as Moshe Feldenkrais stated in his book, *Awareness through Movement: Health Exercises for Personal Growth*. To learn from the powerful, cyclical motion of the ocean's tides is an aspect of salvation—to learn that death follows and is part of life, to learn that joy can rush in when sorrow pervades. A Zen master wrote:

> The waters before, and the waters after;
> Now and forever flowing, follow each other.

We give in to the experience and the events which the myriads of world present to us. Accepting and surrender are more connected with salvation than planning and controlling. It is a psychological and spiritual truth that our misery and unhappiness we plan and program, but our bliss and happiness we do not. The latter occur indirectly, in spite of ourselves, and seem to happen *to* us. Zen and other Eastern traditions would say that salvation is being ready to let good things happen.

Most of us have a knack of making a career out of our limitations. We do this not only in the profession and announcement of our own inadequacies, but also in our clinging to the external forms of tradition found in ritual, doctrines, and church institutions. If we can move out and up in our spiritual lives we can go beyond these limitations. We can live without being anxious about nonperfection and unfulfillment. And we can move beyond church forms that deaden the spirit.

The surprise and spontaneity of living in the myriads of world produces a new spirit. Kanzan, the Zen divine fool, known in Chinese as Han-shan, is bold enough to call such a spirit happiness. In our salvation quest, he bids us live it up!

> Be happy if there's something to be happy about!
> When the moment comes, do not lose it!
> So don't sit there grumbling . . .
> At the end of the Classic Filial Piety
> It tells you what funerals are like.

Kanzan reminds us that there is enough worry and somberness in life anyway. The situation is not unlike that of Jesus when he was criticized for not giving money to the poor and for participating in an act of celebration and anointment. Our Lord said simply, "For you always have the poor with you, and whenever you will, you can do good to them; but you will not always have me" (Mk. 14:7). We are saved by going out and up and expressing our joy.

So often Eastern religions are thought to be passive, inactive, and inward. But, as I reflect upon my experiences of trying to forget the self and to "be enlightened by all things," I am reminded of the Sanskrit word *samyaktva*, the subtle balance of tranquillity and action. Tranquillity is always present in the Eastern stress on meditation. There is a marked difference between prayer and meditation. Meditation is just sitting, just being where we are. In prayer, we extend our being—prayer is a "going." As Bhagwan Sri Rajneesh says, "In prayer you rise like high waves in the ocean to touch the beyond. In meditation you simply wait." It is significant that Jesus said to his disciples in Gethsemane, "Sit here while I *go* yonder and pray" (Matt. 26:36). Eastern religions are concerned more with meditation than with prayer, but this does not mean disassociation and withdrawal. We are active because of our tranquillity. We spring from our meditation into the world—to do, to decide, to love. Furthermore, there is no possible retreat when we truly come to know ourselves, for we know ourselves in a world and surrounded by a world. A critical student of mine once asked a Japanese Zen teacher, "Why do you spend all your time inside doing meditation and following these rituals when outside there is smog, poverty, and crime?" The *roshi*, or teacher, simply replied, "There is no inside or outside—it is all one world." In Zen, at least, there is an abiding connection with "things outside" and a responsibility laid upon those who practice inside. Tranquillity is to be balanced with action.

"To be enlightened by all things" leads me to think of our nuclear arms race. We need to be saved from our judgments of self-righteousness; we need to cast aside our attachment to megatons; we need to move out and up toward a new understanding of our relationship with the Soviet Union. Russia may be our foremost adversary and our political opponent, but Russia is not our enemy. In present international relations we can no longer act on the basis of "mortal enemies." If we do, the end of our mortality is imminent—everybody's mortality. We need to be enlightened by bold new possibilities and new necessities. More especially, we need to remind ourselves that salvation is always concerned with peace, whether we speak from a Christian, a Buddhist, or any other religious perspective. We engage in our practice, worship, and liturgy in order to be at peace, and from this there may come peace in the world. The vision of peace is dim in the frightening and power-mad world of military expenditure. But we who live to be enlightened by all things must keep the vision alive. As Shiki wrote:

> Though it is broken—
> Broken again—
> Still it's there:
> The moon on the water.

JOHN WESTERHOFF

As Christians we proclaim the death of Christ as our salvation. We believe that we are born to die, to die to live. I am just beginning to understand. A few years ago I was asked to preside at an ecumenical Eucharist and to include the major speakers in the liturgy. One of these was a black woman, an Anglican from Johannesburg, South Africa. When I asked her what she would like to contribute to the liturgy, she quickly exclaimed, "I would like to be the crucifer and carry the cross." She did. But when she got to the altar, she froze. As the service proceeded, she slowly raised the cross higher and higher. By the time we came to the Kiss of Peace, tears were streaming down her face. I offered her God's peace and asked, "Is there anything else I can do for you?" She responded, "No, my brother, I have never been more happy in my whole life." I proceeded with the liturgy. After we had processed out of the hall, I approached her and asked, "Can you share with me what happened today?" She answered, "Yes! My brother is the crucifer in our church in Johannesburg. Just before I left, we celebrated our church's saint's day. We were having a procession in the streets, and my brother had refused—he is only ten—to carry his registration card. The police stopped us and because he did not have his card they arrested him. That was three days ago. My priest called last night to tell me that the police had beaten him and that last night he died. I was carrying that cross for him today. Like Jesus, John, my brother, died for God's salvation. Today, as we shared Eucharist, I expressed my thanksgiving for his witness and in the mystery of it all I was united with him and with Christ and with all those in the world through whom God witnesses to his kingdom coming."

That event caused me to ask whether I have seen God's salvation, whether I was witnessing to the world that is to come.

What is the ultimate goal of human life or what Christians speak of as salvation? Nothing is more central to life than the ends for which we humans live and die.

Christians affirm that being human has a source, a potentiality, and a fulfillment which is given by God, offered by God, and secured by God. Being human is not solely at the mercy of time, circumstance, and death. We are saved and fulfilled. The activity of God is God's universal and all-embracing work of bringing about union with God, self, neighbor, and nature. For all human beings we must live in the here and now, in the particular. The ultimate enjoyment of the fullness of God's salvation lies always in the future but it is likewise in each and every present. It is through history that God is building up the ultimate victories of what it means to be human in community.

Salvation for the Christian is historical; it is the assertion that the promised New Age for which all humanity longs is at hand. This kingdom of God or the world to come is a world transformed; it is a world in which the purposes of God's creation have been realized.

For the Christian there can be no duality of worlds into "this world" and "the world beyond." On the contrary, "the world to come" is this world—but transformed, altered and renewed. The hope of salvation is not a hope for a never-never land. It is the fulfillment of our ultimate destiny as humans, the completion of God's original intention in creation.

Thus, salvation is liberation from all that depreciates or negates the wholeness and holiness of individual and corporate life; and it is reconciliation for life in unity with God, humanity, self, and nature. It is the fulfillment of human life, a communal order of peace and justice and productivity under the rule of God, shared in by all peoples and nations.

As H. Richard Niebuhr is said to have replied to a zealous street evangelist who asked him if he was saved: "I was saved by what Christ did: I am being saved right now; I shall be saved when the Kingdom comes." Salvation is a process begun in the saving activities of God in Jesus Christ. It continues into the present as the spirit moves to deliver and make whole. It reaches a climax in God's good time when the purpose of God is realized in human history.

Christianity is faith in the future, in a blessed infinite future of the consummation of God's will for all creation. The Christian looks forward to the future. We are Christian only if we love the future more than the past or the present. We misunderstand if we use eternal life and salvation to glorify or defend our present situation.

The present must always be provisional, something to be conquered; transitory, not our lasting home no matter how pleasant it may appear. A Christian simply cannot be a conservative reactionary. Salvation is not a reward for conserving the present. Nor can we be utopian revolutionaries. We are awaiting a real future that is in God's hands, the consummation of God's deed, the coming of God's kingdom and not the fruit of our labors.

We must worship neither the gods of the present nor of the future we might create. We must contemplatively live in God's future already made present and act humbly with God as advocates and signs of what has come, is coming, and will come. It is a strange way to understand life, but it is Christian. We are not to strive to build on our own the perfect world or even the perfect life. We are to advocate with positive visions and negative prophetic judgments on ourselves and the world in which we live. We are to listen for and look for those places where God is acting in our lives. In the social world, we are to turn negatives into positives and to act with God in those places where we might be a sign of what God is doing. It is a humble life lived in contemplative openness discerning where God is acting so that we might act with God wherever we live and within the great or limited possibilities offered us.

In Christian faith there is a built-in orientation to the future. Jesus proclaimed that God's kingdom was at hand and that its powers are working in the present. In this way he created expectancy. He pointed us toward a future in which the promise of the present world would be fulfilled. But the life of the world to come is not a dream or an ideal to be realized; it is a reality that God is even now creating.

There is a popular erroneous version of Christian life in which heaven is a place or state of being in which people are forever happy and blessed—in which all things are right. Men and women go to this heaven after their death on certain conditions; that is, if they have believed the Gospel and kept God's commandments.

My experiences with Christians in Latin America, however, have helped me to see salvation in terms of a new just society involving the transformation of people not only in terms of cultural values and personal life-styles but in economic and political patterns.

So used are we to thinking in terms of two worlds, this world and the next, the world beyond, that we have devalued human life here and made this world only preparation for the real world.

It isn't enough that we sing or say that Jesus Christ is Lord. We need to be clear about which Jesus we have made decisive in our lives, which Jesus we have made the authority for our faith. For the Christian, it is the Jesus of history; the Jesus with a simple and clear message: there is one God who acts in history and has an intention for creation, namely a world of peace, justice, unity, equity, and the health and well-being of all. Jesus further proclaimed the coming of God's community. He announced that God's cause will, in spite of contrary evidence, prevail; that the future belongs to God. This same Jesus proclaimed one supreme norm for all human life: God's will, which was not a law or laws, but a way of being faithful. God's will, when it is done, will contribute to God's intention for creation. Jesus, therefore, was biased toward those who were denied God's intentions, but he identified himself with all people and their needs. He acted on behalf of the sick, weak, lame, hurt, and oppressed. But he also sought out the heretics, the hypocrites, and the immoral, bringing them both judgment and mercy and thereby converting them to newness of life.

All this was good news and an example of life lived in unity with God and God's will. Still he was killed. But God did not permit his death to end his life. So it was that the little community who followed him and called him Rabbi experienced amidst their doubt that the crucified is living, that his death was dying into God. Jesus, the one seemingly forsaken by God, lives with, through, and in God. Thus, the cross is an event of salvation and the resurrection a witness to God's transforming power.

Piety and politics, religious experience and prophetic action, personal contemplation and social witness are continually pitted against each other, although the Christian faith calls for the integration of inner growth and outer change.

Piety in one sense is a neutral word. Ed Farley, in *Requiem for a Lost Piety*, defines Christian piety as a pattern of being and doing that rises out of a specific interpretation of the Gospel. For some, the Christian life is a privatized, otherworldly, anti-intellectual, emotional affair, which traditionally has been called pietism and is, from my perspective, a misinterpretation of the Gospel. Authentic Christian piety is individual and corporate, otherworldly and this-worldly, intellectual and emotional. Piety without politics is, therefore, barren, while politics without piety is soulless.

The spiritual life then is a historical life lived with a conscious awareness of God's presence; it is life so lived that our minds, hearts, and wills are united with God's in common historical reflective action. Surely this understanding rules out prayer in which the world or the self is depreciated or denied, in which the human personality is dissolved or absorbed into a unity with an otherworldly reality. Prayer is not a negative process moving us out of our normal state or condition, a passive resigned contemplation of otherness, nor a striving after emotional ecstasy through the extinction of thought or volition. Prayer is ultimately an ethical activity. History is the peculiar province of God's revelation and fellowship. Blessedness of life with God is life in this world; in our daily lives we meet and have communion with God.

The Christian life focuses upon the spirit of God in us and in the world; its quest is for an active unity with the God of history. The climax of the Christian life is not enlightenment but unification with the will and activity of God.

A duality of worlds has no place in Christian understanding of life of the world to come. On the contrary the world to come is this world transformed, altered, renewed, reformed. Heaven is not another world, but this present life reformed according to God's will.

Our hope is for a transformed world. The central vision of world history is that all creation is one, every creature in community with every other, living in harmony and

security toward the joy and well-being of every other creature. It is a vision of all people drawn into community
around the will of God for the well-being, health, and
prosperity of all people. It is for a historic, political, economic community, a social order in which justice and peace
are realized and freedom and equity are known. Our spiritual need is being able to discern how God wants us to live
as a saved people called to advocate and be a sign of God's
salvation.

Discernment of spirits is an art and a science of faith.
While the basic principles can be learned rather quickly,
the art of practicing discernment of spirits can only be
learned over a long period. Unless the principles are put
into continuous practice, they will be unprofitable and
soon forgotten. To assist in a personal program of ongoing
discernment, the following practices are proposed: We
need to develop the habit of remaining conscious of our
moods throughout the day and learn to discern their causes and meaning. We need to make preparation for the next
day's prayer each night by an examination of our life
experience. Where is our spirit tending? What need of
prayer is it manifesting? What is it longing to find in
prayer? We need to meditate on the Scriptures each day
and be alert to its leadings. And we need to seek to make
the memory of God's manifestations (graces) in our personal experience a habitual aspect of our prayer life.

Personal memory of God's manifestations to us is the
practice of returning to drink anew at the springs of one's
own first graces, so that old graces may be refreshed, old
powers restored, old commitments reaffirmed, and forgotten knowledge of God renewed. To prayerfully recall a
past grace experience is to discover it has not passed. Daily
we should try to locate, by memory, those deep artesian
wells of grace in our soul that spring up, one for each of
our deepest religious experiences; to locate any one of
these experiences and allow it to grow into the present,

with its whole composite of feelings, moods, thoughts, convictions, commitments, and exceeding joy. We also need to discover how alive and present those experiences still are. For example, we should recall the first awakening to the realization that *God loves me!*; the deepest experience that God forgives me!; the day I found out *You are calling me to follow You!*; the most cherished experience of You in prayer; the most intimate experience of You in the Eucharist; the day and hour I discovered You really are my personal Savior!; my most wonderful finding of You in nature; my most profound discovery of You in another; the most vivid religious dream I've ever had. Another aid to developing discernment skills is through the practice of "childlike" petition. Prayer proceeds contemplatively and intuitionally from awareness of our present affective states or moods. Prayer has the power to change us; but prayer requires our active cooperation. Childish prayer lacks that cooperation. Childish prayer could, for instance, ask God to change me, to remove my disordered affection and attachments, but without any effort on my part. It expects "magic" and does not understand "miracle." For example, if we always feel hostile to Jane or John every time we meet her or him, in our prayer we can enter the presence of God and we can employ memories to invite Jane or John to be present. Immediately we will feel the hostility. Instead of trying to make it subside, we can own the feeling of hostility *before God*, confess our sinfulness and need of help and ask God to burn the hostility away with Christ's love.

Each day we can think of some individual toward whom we have a disordered affection (hatred, hostility, rage, jealousy, disordered love) and enter the presence of God, invite the person to be present in memory, and proceed as above. Or we can think of some *class* from which we are alienated; the world—a racial, social, or economic group—and then proceed as before. Or we can think of some affective state of our own from which we are alienated, perhaps because we consider it weakness (gentleness, reverence), or because we fear our own weakness (tenderness, sweetness), or because we are proud (openness, warmhearted praise of another). We can evoke the feeling, put down the fears, ask God's help to be healed in the likeness of Christ.

Most important is discerning God's Will. To do so we need to be able to develop a proposition. Such proposition should be personal, a concern related to some aspect of our life that we have either neglected to attend to or have not yet successfully settled. We need to develop our concern into a proposition for decision. Of course, we are obliged to study our situation, get all the facts, and rationally consider various possibilities, but that isn't enough. We need to take this proposition into prayer, enter the presence of God conscious of *WE* (of our relationship with God). First offer God the proposition as something you *will do.* Then offer it to God as something you *will not do.* See which pleases God. Be conscious of your own interior feelings and affections. Look for the signs of love, peace, and joy as signs of God's good pleasure; of lovelessness, unrest, and sadness as signs you are taking a wrong turn, perhaps by needlessly burdening yourself. If it feels more like water dripping into a wet sponge than into a hard rock it is God's Will for you. No matter how painful it may be, it will feel "right." If your discernment is successful, be faithful to it.

We also need to find a spiritual director or guide whose role is to listen to our account of the movements of our spirits and confirm or question our discernments.

Praying is a worldly activity, that is, it is what human beings do in the world. Anthony Bloom, in *Living Prayer,* wrote "In our struggle for prayer . . . we must bring to God a complete, firm determination to be faithful to him and strive that God should live in us. We must remember that the fruits of prayer are . . . a deep change in the whole of our personality." The question we must bring to our spiritual life is this: "Is the will of God being realized in my life and in the life of the community?"

The world of human affairs is the theater of God's activity. The realm of God's creating, redeeming, and sanctifying power is the created order. We are called to worship and serve God in the world. Recall Jesus' prayer recorded in John's Gospel: "Father, I do not pray that you take them out of the world, but that you keep them from the evil one."

Christian prayer sees a world in the light of a particular story and vision. Prayer is giving oneself to the Christian story and vision; Discernment is the spiritual life of contemplation and action in the present between memory and vision.

CHAPTER EIGHT

Into the Future
Church Life and Learning

Teaching and learning have become the province of scientific investigation. Scientific positivism and materialism have dominated educational theory. While we do not intend to belittle such efforts or positions we do intend to assert their limited value, especially for Christian nurture. As Erik Erikson has said, knowledge is always tied to the conditions under which it is researched. A scientific investigation of learning is prejudiced by both the world-view or perspective of the investigators who establish the questions to be asked and the methods they choose to secure answers.

While the prestige of scientific investigation is overwhelming in our contemporary world, Thomas Kuhn, the historian of science, in his book *The Structures of Scientific Revolutions*, describes the severe limitations of science and reveals the unsettling fact that often science's most impressive insights prove illusory. Perhaps there is a reality that science cannot adequately investigate and over which it should never have the last word. Perhaps teaching and learning, when they are applied to such a reality, cannot be adequately addressed by scientific method or insight. Our experience leads us to conclude cautiously that such is the case.

We both would assert that our differing spiritual experiences have occurred in unscientific, unpredictable fashion. The reasons and the sources are seldom clear. We are reminded of Basho's *haiku:*

> I know not from what temple
> The wind brings the
> Voice of the bell.

We seem to be aware of the singularity and specialness of each experience. We cannot speak of the spiritual events in our lives as if they were similes—"like" something else which others have had. Rather the imaginative, energy-giving, unique idea of metaphor applies. Each experience seems very much to have its own form and content, crying out for interpretation by the participant. With the power of metaphor, the experience will reach out to others and invite them to share, but the meaning to others will always be indirect and even ambiguous. There is nothing very scientific about our telling. Nor are we very clear about the form or final shape of our spiritual lives, composed of these experiences. We live in the hope expressed by a Zen poem:

> Though we cannot see the Way, it is
>   ever before us:
> Enlightenment is neither near nor far
> And this is all we need to know.

In the preceding chapters we have explored foundational concerns through reflection on our personal experience in the light of a faith community's tradition. Our focus has been the experience of human life in its journey toward fulfillment and on the ways by which persons have learned to be and become fully human. The value of our insights, of course, is related to their correspondence with our experience, with the faith tradition that informs our understandings and ways, and with our own analysis and interpretation.

Our intention in this last chapter is to draw together our

varied insights concerning Christian nurture, especially those which we have discovered make a contribution to the development and growth of the spiritual life. We trust they will prove useful to all who share in our human pilgrimage to integration and fruitful living.

We begin by asserting the central and foundational importance of liturgy and ritual—individual and corporate—for spirituality, indeed for true and fulfilled human life. For some readers this will seem unnecessary to restate, for others it will still appear strange. The church shares with many other institutions religious tasks common to all. The search for truth, the care of the sick and the needy, the struggle for justice and peace are not the sole prerogatives of the church. However, "there remains to the church only one unique and peculiar responsibility: the conduct of public worship"; that was said in 1925 by the one-time Congregational dean of the Divinity School of Harvard University, Willard L. Sperry. He was right, of course. Everything else may be conceded, compromised, shared or even relinquished, but if the church does nothing other than to keep open a house, symbolic of the homeland of the soul, where in season and out women and men come to reenact the memory and vision of who they are, it will have rendered society and each of us a service of unmeasurable value. So long as the church bids men and women to participate in the liturgies of the Christian faith community it need not question its place, mission or influence in the world. If it loses faith or is careless in its rituals it need not look to its avocations to save it.

We think of the structured, ongoing, central practice of *zazen*, or Zen meditation. The bells, clappers, chanting, posture, breathing concentration are a liturgy—always the same, but offering the possibility of each sitting being new and fresh. Zen is nothing without *zazen* and its form.

For those who might question the significance of ritual or liturgy in human life or spiritual formation it would be well to consider the findings of the Religious Experience Research Unit at Manchester College, Oxford. Edward Robinson, in *The Original Vision*, describes the significant religious experiences of children and their close connection with the ceremonial life of the church. Robinson contends and defends the notion that this childhood vision is a form of knowledge and one that is essential to the development of mature understanding. He writes that this early experience is best understood as mystical and religious. We agree. While the liturgy is not educational in the didactic sense, we—all of us, children included—do learn from participation in the community's individual and corporate repetitive symbolic acts expressive of its myth. Through our ritual life, we come to know who we are, we enter into meaningful relationships with God and we experience the gift of community. Christian nurture and the community's liturgies go together; indeed, Christian nurture is best engaged in through the liturgical life of the church.

Without wanting to depreciate the importance of the intellect and the reason, for the human mind cannot know without interpretation, we want to assert our conviction that Christian nurture must take seriously the intuitive way of knowing, the affective mode of thinking, the responsive dimension of consciousness—all of which are nourished and nurtured by the arts. The creation of and participation in music, dance, drama, and visual arts are essential to the spiritual life. Christian nurture needs to both bring persons in touch with great works of art and encourage them to produce their own creations. We should not for a moment think this task easy. Recently money was raised for the creation of a set of altar candelabra, a processional cross, and candles for the Duke University chapel. A large number of divinity school students objected, saying that the money should have been spent for good works. While rightly asserting that our resources should be used for moral ends, they did not understand that goodness, truth, and beauty are related virtues and that without beauty we might not have visions to inspire our theological convictions or moral life. We all know the difficulty faced when churches use the arts with children. Typically, parents wonder why they are not "learning something." Nevertheless, we are more sure than ever that the intuition and the arts are connected and need to become primary and central concerns of Christian nurture if the spiritual life is to be enhanced and enlivened. While our rational consciousness deals in words, concepts, and ideas, our inner lives are generally present to our consciousness in the form of nonverbal images and feelings.

A host of other human possibilities need to be nurtured for the spiritual life. These include emotional expression, visualization and imagination, empathy, creative expression, fantasy and paranormal abilities, such as telepathy and clairvoyance. We all need to learn to be at home with paradox and ambiguity, with risk, surprise, and love of the unpredictable, with liminal experiences, chaos and evil, with mystery and wonder, with solitude and silence. We need to nurture our dreams and visions. We need to accept and to welcome our daydreams—and to learn from them about ourselves. We need to learn to acknowledge the importance of being, at times, dependent, nonproductive, nonrational, and spontaneous.

Edmund Carpenter, the anthropologist, in *Oh, What a Blow That Phantom Gave Me* describes the differences between ocular and oral culture. Ocular culture has a tendency to understand perception singularly as seeing; it comprehends the world through sight. "Seeing is believing." Typically, an ocular culture is a book-oriented culture. Influenced by the characteristics of the eye, an ocular culture tends to see everything flat, in a continuous line of connected cause and effect relationships. Like the eye, it views reality as detached, sees one thing at a time and focuses on the particular by abstracting it from the whole.

While this is a caricature, to be sure, ocular culture can be contrasted with oral. In an oral culture all the senses are involved. Rarely will you find a literalist in an oral story-telling culture. Persons are more involved and not so uncomfortable with dissonance, discontinuity, surprise, or emotion.

It would be fair to say that our North American culture has become increasingly ocular. It is our contention that a healthy spiritual life necessitates the development of touch, taste, learning, sight, and smell—of all the senses—and that the characteristics of an oral storytelling, sensate, emotive, involved culture need to be nurtured in us all. We have discovered the importance of the smell of incense and flowers, the sound of musical instruments and running brooks, the touch of water and of each other's arms, the taste of bread and wine, and the sight of stained-glass windows and flickering candles. We have learned how to be "attuned." We have sensed the greater significance of shared experiences and stories told, in contrast to lectures read.

However, we need to make very clear that the spiritual life is not an evasion of intellectual responsibility. We must acquire a disciplined passion for reason and right thinking about religious experience. The spiritual life is a dialectic between God's self-disclosure and reason. The classical Greek word for right thinking is *paideia*. It means literally "bringing up children," which implies the disciplined education of the mind in both its intellectual and intuitive modes. This is obviously not to defend a sterile or passionless intellectualism, but an affirmation of the unity of heart and head, the affective and cognitive domains of human thought.

The process of spiritual growth is the development of consciousness and the wholeness of human life in moral community. As the late Urban Holmes put it, "The outcome of the experience of God in Christ should be a heightened consciousness which becomes the basis for action which is virtuous." Christian education must support that understanding. Still, a few questions about the processes that lead to that spiritual end are necessary.

As early as 1968, when John Westerhoff was editor of *Colloquy*, he asked John Eusden to write an article entitled "Zen Buddhist Insights for Christian Education." Eusden's thoughts in that essay are even more relevant now. In that piece he had a Zen master ask: Why are you so general? Why do you like to begin talking about ideas—comprehensive and all-pervading? Why do you not rely more on the specific and the concrete in Christian education? The Zen philosopher Kitaro Nishida wrote, "Generalities do not exist apart from the specific; that which is truly general is the latent force in the background of the specific realization. . . ." One will be led to the idea of beauty by contemplating a particular blossom, not by mulling over the form or sense of the idea of beauty. Individual things can speak and point beyond themselves, but they first must be taken at full impact and value. If we would find out what the wind is and what it teaches, we must listen to it and become absorbed in it. We must concentrate on the wind as it is before we go on to think about what it says of emptiness and unity. We need to place ourselves in the midst of the wind's fury and sharpness in a space where the words of Basho's *haiku* will be part of our experience.

> Through jagged cedars rips the winter blast,
> Honed on the craggy ledges as it passed.

The Christian faith is full of enough poignant, provocative specifics to be spoken about directly and bluntly. We need not moralize or theologize about the cross. Talking about the specifics of that death and of that suffering is enough. Let us formulate our own ideas about the meaning of that death. Let us first lose ourselves in the agonizing concreteness of the Son of Man's dying. Let us make use of art!

We should make better use of the close-at-hand in our teaching. The simplest things can help us formulate the ideas of God as Creator and Provider. We Christians over-talk creation. We advance theories, historical and theological, about creation—losing not only wonder, mystery, and awe, but also meaning. As Lao Tzu said, "Meaning is that which exists through itself, always in connection with something." Let us use the most ordinary things in talking about beginning, growth, and change: rocks and water, trees and clouds. In Zen we always concentrate on that which can be experienced, the firefly, not the star—and we let the meaning come from something close by and readily accepted. The simplest happenings and experiences all can contain and express our ideas.

> The wind has stopped
> The current of the mountain stream
> With only a windrow
> Of red maple leaves.

We need to watch the leaves fall into the brook and talk about this imaginatively and at length, and perhaps after some time a great meaning will come through: Nothing lasts forever. A stream once flowing will be clogged and perhaps made stagnant by falling leaves.

We ought not to be afraid of repetition, knowing that there is yet more to be grasped. Far better, we would think, to say over and again to a questioning person, "Christ is risen. Christ is risen," than to give an elaborate and oftentimes confusing explanation of the resurrection. That Christ is risen is *for the person* and it must be known by that person who alone can make the discovery.

We need to use the sudden and the unexpected in our teaching. Again, we are bothered by the discourse, argument, and presentation in Christian education. We believe that the mind can be opened only through an experience that is brisk and startling. Encountering the unexpected through the questioning of a teacher or the discovery of something new in an experience is like seeing a door opening. Or, as a student of Taoism has written, "It is like the gathering of forces within a clock when it comes to strike the hour. The mechanism of the mind seems to have something in common with that of the clock. At a certain moment, in those minds which are prepared for it, the forces of the personality bring themselves together and throw aside the veil that has encircled them, to look out upon a new world about them." We must be ready to provide that unexpected question, observation, or, perhaps, silence that will allow the door to click open or the clock to strike.

We must also consider the body. We Christians are so intellectual. Life is emotional and physical. It would seem important in our worship, for example, to get up and move to a special place, as some do, to receive the bread and wine. We are not rigid about the position of the body in *zazen*, or sitting in meditation, but we do say that this important discipline requires some different and definite posture of the body. If the movement of the hands or the body is involved with emotional participation, it becomes educational.

Perhaps most crucial, we must acknowledge that learning is a process that goes from the inside to the outside. Too often we try to push things into people, and our pushings are brushed aside. Learning is like the process of a chick hatching from an egg; as many Buddhist teachers have pointed out, the chick hatches by pecking from within. A blow from the outside will destroy the hatching process. Many of our programs have little to do with the genuine questions people are asking on the inside. Classes on doctrine and perfunctory study groups are all too often unconnected from the genuine questions and needs of people. We have a statement of such futility: "To look for hair on the back of a tortoise or seek for horns on the head of a rabbit." Often we are chopping a tree to get water, as a Zen master would say.

If we stress the incarnation of "God's presence," we must believe that God is somehow at work in this educational motion from the inside to the outside. We need to encourage people to trust their questions, to be open about them, and to follow their own maturation or hatching process. A disciple once asked a master a question about the nature of the Buddha. The master replied, "Bring me a clean bowl." When the priest-disciple brought the bowl, the master said, "Now put it back where you found it." A true Zen teaching example. The master meant that the priest's questionings must go back to their proper place, the questioner's heart and inner self, where alone true spiritual knowledge can be found.

Urban T. Holmes was among the most intellectually stimulating and creative minds in the field of spiritual theology. In *A History of Christian Spirituality*, he developed a descriptive analysis for a psychology of prayer that we have adopted for the purpose of understanding the various ways by which persons can be nurtured as Christians. Our contention is that a broad understanding of Christian nurture integrates four modes of spiritual life. First is an intellectual, speculative, sensate mode consisting of meditation on Scripture and mental prayer leading to insight, whose heresy is rationalism with its tendency toward dogmatism and an excessive concern for reason and right thinking. Second is a volitional, speculative, nonsensate mode consisting of moral actions and active prayer leading to witness, whose heresy is moralism with its tendency toward a prophetic judgment of culture and excessive concern for right actions. Third is an affective, emotive, sensate mode consisting of pious devotions and affective prayer leading to presence whose heresy is pietism with its tendency toward anti-intellectualism and excessive concern for feelings and right experiences. And fourth is an

intuitive, affective, nonsensate mode consisting of emptying and contemplative prayer leading to mystical union
whose heresy is quietism with its tendency toward neglect
of the social world and an excessive concern for absorp-
tion into God.

Each of us, due to our unique personality, being a combination of heredity and culture, is more at home, at least
in the beginning, in one of these modes. Various "schools
of spirituality" focus on one of the modes, at least in terms
of a point of entry. All should affirm the truth and value
of the others. Each seeks balance and integration. Each
works to counter its own natural heresy. Christian nurture
needs to acknowledge these differences and aid persons
both to fully develop what is most natural for them and
to expand their spiritual life to include the others.

The course we are traveling (often called curriculum)
has multiple understandings. For some it is understood as
an assembly line where persons are molded. Teachers
(adults) are skilled technicians, students (children and
youth) are valuable pieces of raw material. The process is
one of molding this valuable raw material into a predetermined design. For others the course is understood as a
greenhouse where persons grow. Teachers (adults) are wise
gardeners who know what each plant is to be when it is
fully grown, students (children and youth) are seeds. The
process is one of helping each individual seed to reach its
predetermined potential.

Both understandings, when translated into educational
designs, seem to require the formulation of objectives,
strategies to reach them and a means for evaluating suc-
cess. Dorothee Soelle, the theologian, comments in her
book on religious experience, *Death By Bread Alone*, that in
a time when learning theories tend more and more to be
reduced to a technical model informed by physics or biol-
ogy, displaying the framework of the conditions under
which we learn and experience—conditions that are then

researched and put into operation—the idea of journey becomes a necessary countermodel. We agree. Our spiritual journeys have proven to us that the experiences most important in life cannot be derived through a process of input-output. We contend, therefore, that a wiser understanding for Christian nurture and the spiritual life is a pilgrimage comprised of pilgrims of all ages sharing a journey toward wholeness and holiness; aware that there is more to life than meets the eye we search together to find our true lives.

Henri Nouwen once commented that Christian nurture necessitates three things: first, someone who is searching; second, someone who is willing to make her or his life a resource for another; and third, the conviction that if there is to be any knowledge it will come from a source beyond both. This has been our experience also. Curiosity is a human quality. Children are born curious and remain so until they are taught otherwise. Too often, in the name of education, we discourage searching. All too typically in churches, children are encouraged to be passive and receptive to our efforts to give them information about truth. Too frequently we focus our teaching efforts on skills or techniques and neglect sharing our lives. We tend to search for educational methods rather than the more difficult and somewhat threatening responsibilities of revealing our innermost strivings to find the meaning of our own lives. Too often we are tempted to do things to or for children believing that we have the truth they need. We are more convinced than ever that Christian nurture necessitates persons of all ages sharing with each other their strivings which can offer the way and the truth and the life. The spiritual life we all quest for comes, however, as a gift to those who share life together in a community of faith. To that end we need to direct our attention.

To help others on their pilgrimage we need to be compassionate. We need to avoid the temptation to laugh at others' ignorance or limitations, to correct others' errors or to do things to or for others. We rather need to be able to share, to live with others, to be gentle and patient. We do not need to have all the answers, nor need we feel we have arrived. We only need to be able to say, "I have no solutions, but I will not leave you alone in your search." Prepared only by our own discipline of prayer and meditation, we need only ask, "Where do you want to go— would you like me to go with you?" Or, "I am going home—would you like to join me?" In either case, we say, of course, that all of us will have to find our own way. The best guide on a spiritual journey is one who does not need to be helpful or needed, one who does not try to bear the responsibility for another life, but who can leave others in the hands of God—and get a good night's sleep. To be a guide is to avoid expectations or imposition of personal causes; to avoid giving answers, information, advice, solutions, and "help." To be a guide is to be the compassionate Zen master who gives his students a *koan*—a puzzling, short question to be used and wrestled with in meditation—a question that has no easily defined resolution but whose force can lead to "true mind." The process involves a willingness to wait and to encourage persons to get in touch with their own struggles, pains, doubts, questions, and ambiguities. It is a humble responsibility that cannot be learned the way one can learn skills for teaching. It is a responsibility based on the wisdom that the best way to explain a spiritual dimension is to make it possible for someone else to find the same meaning. All one can do is take responsibility for one's own spiritual growth and be willing to be with others as they do likewise. We "teach" others to be spiritual and pray by living with them a life of prayer.

Therefore, we need to be warned against the temptation to teach technique. Learning in the spiritual life is an art and not a science. Worse, idolatry is turning spiritual means into ends. Throughout this book we have alluded to spiritual exercises. None is an end; each is a means of value to some, but not necessarily to all. Most need to be adapted to meet personal needs. At the beginning of our journey the discipline of these exercises will be extremely important; indeed life in the spirit will be hard work. But at the end of the journey we can look forward to living naturally in a continual conscious relationship with God.

Perhaps the essence of what we have discovered in our exploration of the spiritual life and learning is contained in a story of a Jesuit priest's conversation with a Zen Buddhist monk. The priest is said to have asked in Japanese "How do you manage to convey to your novices your spiritual ideas?" The old monk smiled and responded, "Thus far I have been admiring the excellence of your Japanese. If I were blind it would be difficult for me to tell whether or not you were Japanese. And yet this question of yours would have immediately told me you were a Westerner. How can you transmit a religious experience in word? Only by a spiritual contact, by 'rubbing' so to say two persons with each other will the disciple perceive the message." It appears as if one of our most important tasks will be purifying our Western concept of knowledge. Only then will we Christians fully grasp the meaning of learning and the spiritual life.

We need to remember that we each bring an inherited temperament to our pilgrimage, and that we travel with others in tradition-bearing communities. Still we can learn from other pilgrims of other traditions and so we close with a few words about our journey East and West.

Three attitudes toward other faiths are possible. The first is *exclusivism*, in which we emphasize the sole truth of our own tradition and are closed to others. We have found that attitude detrimental to spiritual development. A second is *inclusivism*, in which we are so totally open to all traditions that we lack a personal identity. We have also found this attitude to be without benefit for the spiritual life. A third is *parallelism*, which is founded upon the characteristics of identity and openness. This is the attitude we have found most faithful and beneficial in our spiritual pilgrimage.

Our experience has proved to us the benefits of sharing the spiritual journey with others who have taken different paths. We believe that this meeting of religions is not only an inescapable fact today, but a value for each of us. What unites us is a sacramental view of life, that is, the refusal to separate the seen and the unseen, the material from the spiritual. Together we affirm that the spiritual impinges upon us in the material and the material is the medium of the spiritual. This sacramental view of life affirms that there is one reality that has material and spiritual dimensions.

In the writing of this book we have shared experiences together. Early in our work, we went on a Taoist walk in a forest in the northwest corner of the Berkshires. John Westerhoff sensed a new and different unity with the natural world, discovered other ways of "seeing into" the nature of things, and discovered a special closeness with his colleague, John Eusden, in the silence at the end of the discipline. Toward the close of this joint work, we shared in the Way or Stations of the Cross on the Duke University campus. Eusden grasped afresh the meaning of suffering, reflected on the power of the "stretching out of the arms of love" on the hard wood of the cross, and entered into a special communion with his co-author during the liturgy. We each have found ways to build these and other spiritual exercises into our own disciplines. New insight has emerged from beyond as we searched and shared our lives as a resource for each other. Our faith and spiritual life have grown deeper and stronger through the writing of this book. We pray that those of you who share our journey will be similarly blessed.

Suggested Reading

Bhagavad-Gita (Song of God). New York: Herder and Herder, 1970.

Corless, Roger, *The Art of Christian Alchemy*. New York: Crossroad, 1981.

Cox, Harvey, *Turning East*. New York: Simon and Schuster, 1979.

Dunne, John, *The Way of All the Earth*. New York: Macmillan, 1972.

Edwards, Tilden, *Spiritual Friend*. New York: Paulist, 1980.

Eusden, John, *Zen and Christian*. New York: Crossroad, 1981.

Feldenkrais, Moshe, *Awareness through Movement*. New York: Harper and Row, 1972.

Fenhagen, James, *More Than Wanderers*. New York: Seabury, 1978.

Herrigel, Eugene, *Zen and the Art of Archery*. New York: Random House, 1971.

Holmes, Urban T., *A History of Christian Spirituality*. New York: Seabury, 1980.

I Ching (The Book of Changes) (John Blofeld, trans.). New York: Dutton, 1968.

Jones, Alan, *Journey into Christ*. New York: Seabury, 1977.

Kaltenmarck, Max, *Lao-Tsu and Taoism*. Stanford, CA: Stanford Univ. Press, 1969.

Kapleau, Philip, *Three Pillars of Zen.* New York: Doubleday, 1980.

Kelsey, Morton, *Transcend.* New York: Crossroad, 1981.

Lao-Tzu, *Tao Te Ching (The Way and Its Power).* New York: Penguin Books, 1972.

Leech, Kenneth, *True Prayer.* London: Sheldon, 1980.

Leonard, George B., *Aikido* and the Mind of the West," *Intellectual Digest,* June 1973.

Macquarrie, John, *Paths in Spirituality.* New York: Harper and Row, 1972.

Merton, Thomas, *Contemplation in a World of Action.* Garden City, NY: Image, 1973.

Nouwen, Henri, *The Way of the Heart.* New York: Seabury, 1981.

Rajneesh, Bhagwan Sri, *Tao: The Pathless Path.* New York: Wisdom Garden Books, 1981.

Snyder, Gary, *Back Country.* New York: New Directions, 1968.

Suzuki, Shunryu, *Zen Mind: Beginner's Mind.* New York: John Weatherhill, 1970.

Turner, Victor, *The Ritual Process.* Ithaca, NY: Cornell Univ. Press, 1977.

Welch, Holmes, *Taoism: The Parting of the Way.* Boston: Beacon, 1966.